QUESTIONS AND ANSWERS
ON FOOD AND BEVERAGE SERVICE

QUESTIONS AND ANSWERS ON FOOD AND BEVERAGE SERVICE

Third edition

Dennis R. Lillicrap MHCIMA, MCFA.SG, *Dip Ed.* . . . .
Senior Lecturer, Department of Hotel and Catering Operations,
Polytechnic of West London

John A. Cousins FHCIMA, FCFA, DMS, MBA . . . .
Head of Department of Hotel and Catering Management,
Polytechnic of West London

Hodder & Stoughton
LONDON SYDNEY AUCKLAND

British Library Cataloguing in Publication Data
Lillicrap, Dennis R.
  Questions and answers on food and beverage service.
  I. Title II. Cousins, John
  647.9507

  ISBN 0–340–55780–X

First published 1988

© 1991 D. R. Lillicrap and J. Cousins

Typeset by Wearside Tradespools, Boldon, Tyne and Wear.
Printed in Great Britain for the educational publishing division of Hodder & Stoughton Ltd, Mill Road, Dunton Green, Sevenoaks, Kent by St Edmundsbury Press Ltd.

CONTENTS

Acknowledgements 6
Introduction 7
1 The food and beverage service industry 8
2 Food and beverage service areas and equipment 17
3 The menu, menu knowledge and accompaniments 29
4 Beverages – Non–alcoholic and alcoholic 53
5 The food and beverage service sequence 72
6 The service of breakfast and afternoon tea 93
7 Specialised forms of service 99
8 Guéridon service 104
9 Function catering 110
10 Supervisory aspects of food and beverage service 117
11 Competence in food and beverage service 133

ACKNOWLEDGEMENTS

The revision of this book has been based on changes within the qualification structures of a variety of examining and award making bodies including HCIMA, City and Guilds and BTEC. The authors would like to acknowledge the assistance given to them by a variety of people and in particular the Food and Beverage Service and Food Studies staff of the Ealing and Slough campuses of the Polytechnic of West London.

INTRODUCTION

This book aims to provide a variety of revision questions on food and beverage service. Although it is based on our text book *Food and Beverage Service* (an 'answer reference' is given after each question indicating where that specific information may be found), it can also be used independently as answers to questions are given at the end of each chapter. Additionally Chapter 11 contains examples of competence statements.

It is our view that those seeking to strive towards excellence in food and beverage service require a combination of practical knowledge and skills, interpersonal skills and product knowledge. The questions posed in this book therefore reflect this belief. Overall we have attempted to provide a testing and revision mechanism for those who wish to measure some of their aquisition of knowledge and skills related to food and beverage service.

1. THE FOOD AND BEVERAGE SERVICE INDUSTRY
(p1–21)

1   Good personal hygiene would be indicated in a food service operator by

   a. well-pressed uniform, clean shoes, unshaven

   b. excessive make-up, well starched apron, hair tied back

   c. clean hands and nails, use of a deodorant, well groomed hair

   d. body odour, excessive jewellery, frequently washed hair   *p17 1.8*

2   When the food service operator is not serving guests they should stand discreetly by their sideboard and

   a. look attentive

   b. watch and anticipate the guests requirements

   c. be ready to assist their colleagues

   d. check they have sufficient equipment in their sideboard to continue the service   *p18 1.8*

3   Should a guest make a minor complaint, the food service operator will

   a. immediately refer the complaint to the superior

   b. offer a discount on the guest's bill

   c. listen tactfully and enter in the complaints book at conclusion of service

   d. rectify the complaint as far as is possible and then inform the superior   *p19 1.8*

4   All food service staff should wear sensible shoes because

   a. they do not wear out so quickly

   b. the guests find them more fashionable

   c. they are more hygienic

   d. it prevents accidents   *p17 1.8*

5   The main reason why the food service operator must have a
    good knowledge of all the menu and wine list items is

    a. so that the correct cover can be laid

    b. so that the food service operator can advise and offer
        suggestions to the guest

    c. because the food and drink cheques must be written out
        correctly

    d. so that the appropriate accompaniments may be
        offered   *p17 1.8*

6   The main reason a good memory is an essential attribute of a
    food service operator is because

    a. it may create a good working relationship between the staff
        and the guest

    b. it ensures the food service operator remembers who has
        ordered each main course dish

    c. it enables more guests to be served within a limited space of
        time

    d. they will always be on duty punctually   *p18 1.8*

7   What is the correct order of seniority of the following four
    members of staff who work together on a station?

    1. chef de rang   a. 1   2   3   4
                                b. 2   1   4   3
    2. station head waiter
                                c. 2   3   1   4
    3. debarrasseur   d. 3   1   4   2

    4. commis de rang   *p14 1.7*

8   The chef de salle is responsible for

    a. lounge service

    b. floor service

    c. banquet service

    d. restaurant service   *p15 1.7*

9 A commis de rang would be an assistant to a
   a. debarrasseur
   b. trancheur
   c. sommelier
   d. chef de rang   *p14 1.7*

10 A chef de rang might be described as
   a. a wine waiter
   b. a station waiter
   c. a floor waiter
   d. the trainee or apprentice   *p14 1.7*

11 The person who has overall responsibility for the service of food
   and drink to guests is
   a. the maître d'hôtel
   b. the aboyeur
   c. the chef de cuisine
   d. the sous chef   *p13 1.7*

12 In a large hotel the person who has overall responsibility for the
   food and beverage department is
   a. the food and beverage manager
   b. the banqueting manager
   c. the duty manager
   d. the restaurant manager   *p12 1.7*

13 Which is the odd one out?
   a. chef d'étage
   b. chef de salle
   c. chef de partie
   d. chef de rang   *p12/16 1.7*

14 Which is the odd one out?

   a. station head waiter

   b. chef de rang

   c. demi-chef de rang

   d. sommelier   *p12/15 1.7*

15 The maître d'hôtel is the French term for the

   a. head waiter

   b. hotel manager

   c. cocktail barman

   d. restaurant cashier   *p13 1.7*

16 The demi-chef de rang is the

   a. carver

   b. apprentice

   c. assistant station waiter

   d. banqueting waiter   *p14 1.7*

17 A sommelier should have a good sense of urgency because he/she

   a. must serve as many guests as possible over the meal period

   b. has to ensure all drink is served before the end of the meal

   c. will achieve maximum commission on sales

   d. should achieve maximum sales of drink over the service period   *p19 1.8*

18 The correct attitude of the food service operator is determined by

   a. being servile

   b. dealing with complaints when time allows

   c. anticipating the guests' needs and wishes

   d. being lax in your work   *p18 1.8*

19 The style of service normally expected to be found in a cafeteria would be

    a. silver service

    b. plate service

    c. self service

    d. guéridon service   *p10 1.6*

20 The trancheur is the French term for the

    a. carving trolley used in the restaurant

    b. the chef who controls the hot plate at service time

    c. the food service operator in charge of a station

    d. the chef who carves at the buffet   *p14 1.7*

21 The French term for the floor waiter is

    a. chef de salle

    b. chef de rang

    c. chef d'étage

    d. debarrasseur   *p15 1.7*

22 Guéridon service indicates that

    a. all the dishes on the menu are individually priced

    b. a meal is served by placing the potato and vegetable dishes on the table for the guest to help himself

    c. a meal is served to a guest on a tray in the room

    d. a meal is served to a guest by the waiter from a trolley or sidetable   *p10 1.6*

23 The techniques and skills of flambée work, carving, filleting and making salad dressings are usually incorporated in

    a. buffet service

    b. guéridon service

    c. carvery service

    d. family service   *p10 1.6/p273 8.1*

24 Which of the following styles of food service would be offered
where rapid turnover of custom and a speedy service is
required?

a. silver service

b. French service

c. family service

d. plate service   *p10 1.6*

25 The style of food service usually found in a carvery is

a. a combination of waiter and self service

b. plate service only

c. plate and silver service

d. full silver service only   *p10 1.6*

26 Which of the following methods of food service would be used
when operating a call-order unit?

a. silver service

b. family service

c. plate service

d. service à la française   *p10/11 1.6*

27 Which of the following styles of food service demands more
skill, dexterity and flair from the food service operator?

a. guéridon service

b. silver service

c. plate service

d. self service   *p10 1.6*

28 Indicate six factors which help to determine the style of service
to be carried out in a catering establishment   *p9 1.6*

29 List four sectors of the industry where one would find counter
or cafeteria service   *p3 1.3/p199 5.4*

30 Two terms which indicate different forms of layout for counter
service are e. . . . . . and f. . .f. . .   *p10 1.6*

31   The sommelier serves all forms of alcoholic beverages during the service of meals in a restaurant   *TRUE/FALSE*   *p15 1.7*

32   The French term for the floor waiter is the C. . . d'é. . . .   *p15 p15 1.7*

33   Any banqueting waiter required to serve a dinner would normally be engaged on a casual basis, as and when necessary   *TRUE/FALSE*   *p16 1.7*

34   List six qualities you would look for in a good food service operator   *p17/18/19 1.8*

35   A pleasant p. . . . . means the waiters will be tactful, courteous, even tempered, well spoken, have good social skills and have the ability to smile   *p18 1.8*

36   The s. . . . . is responsible for the service of all alcoholic beverages during the service of meals   *p15 1.7*

37   The lounge waiter is responsible for the service of afternoon teas   *TRUE/FALSE*   *p15 1.7*

38   Where does the chef d'étage normally work from?   *p15 1.7*

39   What is the definition of the restaurant term 'station'?   *p14 1.7*

40   Which member of the restaurant staff must ensure close liaison and cooperation with the housekeeping staff to effect efficient service?   *p15 1.7*

41   The station head waiter and station waiters work from which item of furniture found in the dining area?   *p14 1.7*

42   List four factors which help determine that the barperson is doing his/her job as a 'salesperson' correctly   *p17–19 1.8/p15 1.7*

43 A food service operator with good social skills should be able to

a. talk diplomatically

b. smile

c. display a sense of humour

d. be familiar

e. be well mannered

f. communicate and be understood

Which is the odd one out?   *p17 1.8*

44 You are preparing a training session for your staff, the aim of which is to emphasise what influences customers in their choice of restaurant, and their satisfaction of the service given. List and briefly explain

a. *three* of the most common factors an adult customer takes into account when choosing a restaurant for a social occasion   *p7/8 1.5*

b. *three* of the most important factors that influence an adult customer's satisfaction in relation to the *service* received   *p9 1.5*

Answers . . . .

1 c,   2 b,   3 d,   4 d,   5 b,   6 a,   7 b,   8 a,   9 d,   10 b,
11 a,   12 a,   13 c,   14 d,   15 a,   16 c,   17 d,   18 c,
19 c,   20 d,   21 c,   22 d,   23 b,   24 d,   25 a,   26 c,   27 a

28   type of customer, time available, anticipated turnover, type of menu, cost of menu, site of establishment

29   Industrial catering; welfare catering; department stores; motorway service stations

30   Échelon – freeflow

31   True

32   Chef d'étage

33   True

34   Personality; attitude; personal hygiene; punctuality; local knowledge; memory

35   Personality

36   Sommelier

37   True

38   Floor pantry/central kitchen

39   Sideboard from which you work and the tables you are responsible for

40   The chef d'étage or floor waiter

41   The sideboard

42   Sense of urgency/appearance/personal hygiene/technical knowledge and skills/sales ability/conduct/attitude/personality

43   d

44   a. physiological, economic, social; psychological, convenience

     b. food and drink, level of service, level of cleanliness & hygiene; value for money/price, atmosphere

2. FOOD AND BEVERAGE SERVICE AREAS AND EQUIPMENT
(p 22–59)

1 The most commonly used material in dining room furniture is

   a. aluminium

   b. brass

   c. plastics

   d. wood   *p44 2.10*

2 A round table 1 metre (3 feet) in diameter is large enough to seat

   a. two guests

   b. three guests

   c. four guests

   d. six guests   *p46 2.10*

3 A restaurant sideboard is used to

   a. store all the glassware that may be required during the meal service

   b. hold all the equipment required by service staff at the commencement of service

   c. store all proprietary sauces that may be required during the meal service

   d. give a visual display of specialist restaurant equipment   *p46 2.10*

4 The exchange of restaurant linen on a one-for-one basis means

   a. one clean for one dirty

   b. one complete set of restaurant linen after each meal service is finished

   c. one exchange each day

   d. one exchange on receipt of one authorised signature   *p47 2.11*

5   The size of tablecloth required to fit a table approximately 76cm (2′6″) square should be

   a. 1m × 1m (36″ × 36″)

   b. 183cm × 183cm (72″ × 72″)

   c. 137cm × 137cm (54″ × 54″)

   d. 244cm × 244cm (96″ × 96″)   *p48 2.11*

6   Which of the following terms denotes that hotel china meets the British Standard 4034?

   a. vitreous

   b. vitrified

   c. ironstone

   d. stoneware   *p50 2.12*

7   When purchasing china which of the following is the *main key factor* that should be borne in mind?

   a. the pattern should be under the glaze

   b. delivery time

   c. the china has been fired at least three times

   d. it is suitable for use in a dishwasher   *p49 2.12*

8   The approximate size of a fish plate is

   a. 15cm (6in)

   b. 25cm (10in)

   c. 18cm (7in)

   d. 20cm (8in)   *p51 2.12*

9   The capacity of a demi-tasse is

   a. 9.47cl (3⅓ fluid ounces)

   b. 18.93cl (6⅔ fluid ounces)

   c. 23cl (8 fluid ounces)

   d. 28.4cl (½ pint)   *p51 2.12*

10   The term 'tableware' indicates

a.   all items of equipment required to lay up a table

b.   all items of cutlery, flatware and hollow-ware

c.   all varieties of china used in the catering trade

d.   all varieties of glassware suitable for serving drinks
     in   *p52 2.13*

11   The British Standard related to the quality of silver-plated
     tableware and stainless steel is

a.   EPNS

b.   18/8

c.   BS 5577

d.   BS 4034   *p53 2.13*

12   Good quality British tableware, made of stainless steel, is
     guaranteed by which of the following markings?

a.   Steelite

b.   20 years plate

c.   A1

d.   18/8   *p53 2.13*

13   The most suitable glass for the service of champagne is

a.   tulip

b.   Elgin

c.   Paris

d.   Wellington   *p56 2.14*

14   Which of the following has only two prongs?

a.   oyster fork

b.   pastry fork

c.   snail fork

d.   fruit fork   *p55 2.13*

15   Match the following glasses to their correct capacities

   a. Paris goblet   (1) 34cl (12 fluid ounces)

   b. Elgin liqueur   (2) 14.20cl (5 fluid ounces)

   c. Worthington   (3) 2.367cl ('6 out')

   d. beer tankard   (4) 28.40cl (10 fluid ounces)   *p57 2.14*

16   It is generally recognised that the Service Area is comprised of which of the following working units?

   a. stillroom – silver room – wash up – hotplate – spare linen store

   b. stillroom – plateroom – wash up – hotplate – plonge

   c. plonge – spare linen store – hot plate – silver room – stillroom

   d. stillroom – silver room – plateroom – wash up – spare linen store   *p24 2.1*

17   Which of the following groups of equipment is most likely to be found in the stillroom?

   a. butter machine – tea dispenser – burnishing machine – refrigerator – still set

   b. butter machine – still set – salamander – gas ring – refrigerator

   c. still set – salamander – bratt pan – hot cupboard – butter machine

   d. hot cupboard – storage cupboards – double sinks and draining boards – guéridon – butter machine   *p25 2.2*

18   Melba toast is prepared in the

   a. larder

   b. kitchen

   c. stillroom

   d. pantry   *p25 2.2*

19 Melba toast is

    a. offered as an accompaniment with pâté maison

    b. only served with breakfast and afternoon tea

    c. offered as an accompaniment with all forms of fruit melba

    d. offered as an alternative to breadrolls   *p26 2.2*

20 The person who controls the hotplate at service time is known as the

    a. aboyeur

    b. chef de rang

    c. chef de partie

    d. trancheur   *p31 2.5*

21 The function of the 'off board' is to inform the staff

    a. at what times they may go off duty

    b. when dishes on the menu are no longer available

    c. when their days off are due

    d. which tables are no longer in use   *p31 2.5*

22 A polivit plate would be correctly used to

    a. serve special fish dishes

    b. clean wood block flooring

    c. clean silver

    d. heat food in a microwave   *p29 2.3*

23 In full silver service who does the waiter collect food from at the hotplate?

    a. aboyeur

    b. chef de partie

    c. trancheur

    d. chef de cuisine   *p31 2.5*

24 Plates which have been washed in a washing up machine should
be

a. stacked and dried in the hotplate

b. dried with a linen cloth

c. dried with a disposable material

d. allowed to air dry   p30 2.4

25 The plate room is an ancilliary department where

a. silver is cleaned and stored

b. china is cleaned and stored

c. glassware is cleaned and stored

d. all the washing up is done   p27 2.3

26 The term 'baveuse' relates to

a. a method of making coffee

b. omelettes

c. grilled steaks

d. salad dressings   p32 2.5

27 The abrasive agent used in a burnishing machine in conjunction
with water and a detergent would be

a. starch

b. bleach

c. steel ball bearings

d. lead shot   p28 2.3

28 A polivit plate is

a. a form of reinforced china

b. a form of hotplate used on a buffet

c. used to reflect heat in a microwave oven

d. an aluminium metal sheet   p29 2.3

29 The hot water in a sterilising tank should be maintained at a temperature of

a. 75°C

b. 85°C

c. 65°C

d. 55°C   *p30 2.4*

30 The term used to indicate a steak required to be cooked 'medium' is

a. saignant

b. à point

c. baveuse

d. bien cuit   *p32 2.5*

31 What is silver dip best used in when cleaning silver?

a. an enamel container

b. a stainless steel container

c. a plastic container

d. a glass container   *p29 2.3*

32 In a carvery operation joints would normally be placed in a hot closet where they would be held at a temperature of about

a. 70–74°C (150–160°F)

b. 74–78°C (160–170°F)

c. 78–82°C (170–180°F)

d. 82–86°C (180–190°F)   *p33 2.5*

33 In full silver service the waiter works from

a. the sideboard

b. the guéridon

c. the buffet

d. the hotplate   *p46 2.10*

34   The definition of the term 'restaurant brigade' is

    a. all the staff who work together in one shift

    b. all the staff who work together on one station

    c. the management team responsible for supervision of the restaurant

    d. the team of trainees learning their trade   *p30 2.4*

35   A paper 'coaster' refers to a

    a. speciality cocktail

    b. a disposable tray cloth

    c. type of mixed beer drink

    d. glass mat   *p36 2.7*

36   One of the main factors which assists in defining the traditional dispense bar is that

    a. only chance customers may be served

    b. it only dispenses wine or other alcoholic drinks to guests consuming a meal

    c. both chance and resident guests may be served

    d. it is open 24 hours a day   *p34 2.7*

37   Indicate four factors which determine that a wine glass is suitable for use in 'tasting' wine   *p56 2.14*

38   Name three pieces of equipment which would come under each of the following headings

    a. Cutlery

    b. Flatware

    c. Hollow-ware   *p52 2.13*

39   The new British Standard introduced in 1978 for silver plated tableware specified two grades known as S....... for general use and R......... for restaurant use   *p53 2.13*

40 List six factors to be borne in mind when purchasing equipment for a food and beverage service area   *p23 2.1*

41 For safety reasons restaurant china should be stored at a c . . . . h . . . . . for placing on, and removing from, the shelves   *p51 2.12*

42 What would a slip cloth be used for?   *p48 2.11*

43 What does the term 'banquette' relate to?   *p45 2.10*

44 How would you define the term 'atmosphere'?   *p23 2.1/p9 1.5*

45 When ordering supplies from the dry goods store for use in the stillroom, what commercial document would be used, and how many copies are there?   *p24 2.2*

46 List ten perishable food items issued from the stillroom   *p25 2.2*

47 What is the definition of the term 'gristick'?   *p26 2.2*

48 Indicate briefly how Melba toast should be made   *p26 2.2*

49 List six pre-portioned items that may be offered from the stillroom.   *p26 2.2*

50 Plate powder should be mixed with methylated spirit rather than water to form a paste?   *TRUE/FALSE*   *p29 2.3*

51 Indicate the degrees of cooking for a grilled steak as shown by the following terms

   1 à point   3 bleu
   2 saignant   4 bien cuit   *p32 2.5*

52 Dirty linen from the spare linen store is normally exchanged on the basis of 'o . . c . . . .' for 'o . . d . . . .'   *p47 2.11*

53 All food orders handed to the aboyeur should be l . . . . . . so that there is m . . . . . . d . . . . in 'calling up' a particular dish   *p32 2.5*

54 Who is responsible for the ordering of supplies from the dry goods store for use in the stillroom?   *p24 2.2*

55 A form of food and beverage service which supplements other systems might often be a . . . . v *p39 2.8*

56 Name the two items of specialist equipment shown in the photograph on page 55 of Food and Beverage Service that would be found on the fruit basket   *p54 2.13*

57 List six key points which might assist in attracting the potential customer into your establishment   *p23 2.1*

58 List six factors which are important considerations in the planning of a bar   *p37/38 2.7*

59 Name the glasses shown

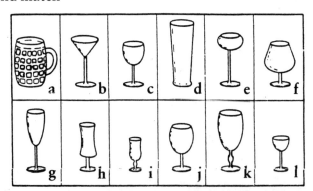

       p56 2.14

60 The correct choice of furnishings and equipment is one of the key factors in promoting a . . . . in your food service area   *p23 2.1*

61 Name ten different types of glassware you might expect to find in a typical bar   *p56 2.14*

62 Mix and match

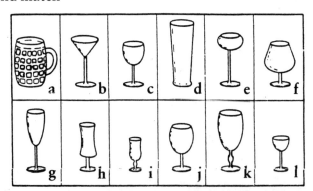

As the dispense barman, in which of the above glasses would you serve the drinks listed below? You may use each of the glasses and drinks listed only once. *Mix and match* the correct glass to the correct drink

drink	glass	drink	glass
Pol Roger		Courvoisier	
Piesporter		draught beer	
Amontillado		gin and bitter lemon	
tawny port		Château Margaux	
Screwdriver		Worthington	
Drambuie		lager	

Answers . . . .

1 d,   2 c,   3 b,   4 a,   5 c,   6 b,   7 a,   8 d,   9 a,   10 b,
11 c,   12 d,   13 a,   14 c,   15 a–2 b–3 c–1 d–4,   16 a,
17 b,   18 c,   19 d,   20 a,   21 b,   22 c,   23 a,   24 d,
25 a,   26 b,   27 c,   28 d,   29 a,   30 b,   31 c,   32 c,
33 a,   34 a,   35 d,   36 b

37   Plain and clear;   has a stem;   slight incurving lip;   large enough to appreciate the wine being tasted

38   *Cutlery:* joint knife, side knife, fish knife;   *Flatware:* soup spoon, sweet spoon, fish fork;   *Hollow ware:* teapot, milk jug, soup tureen;   or any suitable alternatives to the above

39   Standard;   Restaurant

40   Design;   colour;   durability;   maintenance;   storage;   breakage;   or any suitable alternatives to the above

41   Convenient height

42   Covering a soiled/grubby tablecloth, and, if coloured, to promote atmosphere

43   Restaurant seating – a style/design of chair

44   The 'feeling' or 'mood' of an establishment on entering and determined by a combination of factors such as lighting, decor, music, staff, and so on

45   Requisition sheet;   two

46 Milk; cream; butter; preserves; cheese biscuits; sugars; fresh fruit juice; bread; Melba toast; rolls/croissants

47 Italian breadstick

48 Toast a slice of bread. Trim crusts. Cut slice horizontally making two slices. Remove surplus dough. Toast the untoasted sides.

49 Preserve; butter; cream; cheese; dry cheese biscuits; cereals

50 True

51 medium 2 underdone 3 rare 4 well done

52 'one clean' for 'one dirty'

53 Legible; minimum delay

54 Head stillroom person

55 Automatic vending

56 Grape scissors, nut crackers

57 Furnishings; design; colour scheme; interpersonal skills; lighting and music; layout and equipment; the menu

58 Area; layout; plumbing; power; safety and hygiene; site/position

59 a. Tulip/flute; b. Hock/Moselle; c. 12fl.oz. short stem Worthington; d. Brandy balloon; e. Pilsner lager; f. Elgin liqueur

60 Atmosphere

61 Elgin sherry; Elgin liqueur; port; brandy; pilsner; wellington; cocktail; Paris goblet; beer tankards; Hock/Moselle

62 a. draught beer b. Screwdriver c. gin and bitter lemon
d. lager e. Piesporter f. Courvoisier g. Pol Roger
h. Amontillado i. Drambuie j. Château Margaux
k. Worthington l. tawny port

3. THE MENU, MENU KNOWLEDGE AND ACCOMPANIMENTS
(p60–100, F&B)

1 The name Duke Henry of Brunswick has connections with

   a. a classical meat garnish

   b. the origins of the menu

   c. an old established brewery company

   d. the French classical menu   *p61 3.1*

2 Which of the following does not indicate a style of menu?

   a. à la carte

   b. table d'hôte

   c. plat du jour

   d. carte du jour   *p70 3.1*

3 Which of the following points relates to an à la carte menu?

   a. a set price per cover

   b. all dishes available at a set time

   c. a limited number of courses

   d. an extensive choice of dishes   *p70 3.1*

4 Which of the following group of factors identifies a table d'hôte menu?

   a. a set price, 3/4 courses, limited choice within each course

   b. dishes individually priced, 3/4 courses, all dishes available at a set time

   c. selling price of the menu is fixed, all dishes available at a set time, an extensive choice

   d. dishes prepared to order, a waiting time, dishes individually priced   *p69 3.1*

5 The term 'plat du jour' normally indicates a

   a. first course dish   c. sweet dish

   b. main course dish   d. speciality coffee   *p70 3.1*

6   Which of the following is considered to be the 'rest' between courses in the French classical menu?

a. relevé

b. légumes

c. sorbet

d. entrée   *p66 3.1*

7   The term 'dessert' classically indicates

a. savoureux

b. entremets

c. plat de fromages

d. corbeille des fruits   *p68 3.1*

8   How many courses normally make up the classic menu sequence in a recognised top class hotel?

a. 13

b. 15

c. 17

d. 11   *p62 3.1*

9   The first main meat course in the classic menu sequence is

a. rôti

b. entrée

c. relevé

d. poisson   *p65 3.1*

10 A luxury restaurant will normally offer to its guests a choice of dishes from

a. the banquet menu

b. an à la carte menu

c. a fork buffet menu

d. the table d'hôte menu   *p70 3.1*

11   Russian cigarettes were traditionally offered with

    a. port

    b. fromage

    c. coffee

    d. the sorbet   *p66 3.1*

12   Which one of the following is classified on the menu as an hors
    d'oeuvre?

    a. truite fumée

    b. sole colbert

    c. scampi frit

    d. homard Newburg   *p63 3.1*

13   The correct sequence of courses for dinner is

    a. potage – hors-d'oeuvre – entrée – savoureux

    b. potage – poisson – rôti – entremets

    c. hors-d'oeuvre – entrée – poisson – légumes

    d. poisson – savoureux – relevé – entremets   *p63/67 3.1*

14   Which one of the following groups is the correct order of
    sequence at a banquet?

1 entremets	a.	6–3–5–2–4–1
2 sorbet	b.	3–5–2–6–4–1
3 poisson		
4 rôti	c.	6–5–3–4–1–2
5 entrée	d.	5–3–6–4–1–2
6 potages		

                                                    p62/68 3.1

15   A full à la carte menu would usually be offered

    a. in a café

    b. in a 5 star restaurant

    c. at a banquet

    d. in a coffee shop   *p70 3.1*

16 Who would normally be responsible for the compilation of the menu?

a. chef de partie

b. chef de cuisine

c. chef d'étage

d. chef de rang   *p61 3.1*

17 The French menu term 'cabillaud' denotes

a. haddock

b. plaice

c. cod

d. lemon sole   *p75 3.2*

18 A guest asks you if there is any shellfish on the menu. What would your answer be if the following menu items are available?

a. fletan poché

b. blanchailles

c. raie au beurre noir

d. cocktail de crevettes roses   *p75 3.2*

19 Which is the odd one out?

a. hareng

b. barbue

c. plie

d. aiglefin   *p75 3.2*

20 A guest requests a lobster dish from your menu. Which of the following terms indicates this to the 'station waiter'?

a. langouste

b. homard

c. huître

d. coquille St Jacques   *p76 3.2*

21 Which of the following omelette dishes would be served 'flat' rather than 'folded'?

a. omelette fines herbes

b. omelette espagnole

c. omelette aux fromage

d. omelette aux jambon   *p64 3.1*

22 'Escalope' is a French menu term normally relating to

a. veal

b. pork

c. mutton

d. beef   *p80 3.2*

23 Which of the following terms denotes a type of 'feathered game'?

a. poussin

b. bécassine

c. oie

d. lièvre   *p76 3.2*

24 Pheasant is in season from

a. September to January

b. April to July

c. October to February

d. March to September   *p76 3.2*

25 Which of the following vegetables is classified as a 'root' vegetable?

a. haricot vert

b. épinard

c. fève

d. rutabaga   *p76 3.2*

26 Which of these groups of fresh fruit is most suitable for the menu dish known as corbeille des fruits?

   a. ananas, Conference, Beauty of Bath, pêche

   b. ananas, Doyenne du Comice, Blenheim orange, framboise.

   c. fraise, Louise Bonne of Jersey, cerise, Bramley Seedling

   d. Newton Wonder, abricot, Worcester Pearmain, airelle rouge   *p77 3.2*

27 Aubergine is used in the preparation of

   a. paella

   b. omelette surprise

   c. moussaka

   d. canneloni   *p78 3.2*

28 The term 'fond' relates to which of the following vegetables?

   a. mais

   b. artichaut

   c. poireaux

   d. topinambour   *p78 3.2*

29 After processing, pimento and chillies produce

   a. paprika and black pepper

   b. cayenne pepper and bay leaves

   c. sage and thyme

   d. paprika and cayenne pepper   *p79 3.2*

30 Flageolets are a type of

   a. haricot bean

   b. broad bean

   c. French bean

   d. runner bean   *p78 3.2*

31 Which of the following pairs of items would you expect to accompany the menu dish 'fromages assortis'?

a. radis/céleri-rave

b. ananas/radis

c. grapes/dessert apple

d. céleri/radis   *p76 3.2/p95 3.4*

32 Grouse is in season from

a. 12 August

b. 1 September

c. 1 October

d. All year round   *p76 3.2*

33 Which one of the following French menu terms denotes a Spring chicken?

a. dinde

b. poussin

c. pintade

d. poulet   *p76 3.2*

34 Which of the following should *not* be classified as a 'flat fish'?

a. turbot

b. raie

c. anguille

d. plie   *p75 3.2*

35 One of the following is incorrectly classified as an 'oily fish'. Which one?

a. blanchailles

b. hareng

c. merlan

d. barbue   *p75 3.2*

36 Fresh broccoli would normally be in season from

    a. April   c. August

    b. June   d. October   *p76 3.2*

Hors-d'oeuvre and substitutes

37 Oil and vinegar is the accepted accompaniment with

    a. les crevettes roses

    b. salade verte

    c. hors-d'oeuvre

    d. huîtres   *p83 3.3*

38 Which of the following items of equipment is used in the presentation of hors-d'oeuvre?

    a. timbale

    b. sur le plat

    c. petit marmite

    d. ravier   *p83 3.3*

39 With which of the following dishes is Worcestershire sauce *not* an accompaniment?

    a. huîtres

    b. Irish stew

    c. jus de tomate

    d. croûte Derby   *p84 3.3*

40 The four accompaniments making up an 'Oyster Cruet' are

    a. peppermill, Worcestershire sauce, lemon, brown bread and butter

    b. cayenne pepper, peppermill, tabasco sauce, chilli vinegar

    c. cayenne pepper, peppermill, half lemon, chilli vinegar

    d. peppermill, tabasco sauce, chilli vinegar, brown bread and butter   *p84 3.3*

41 With which of the following 'starter' dishes should a waiter *not* offer hot breakfast toast?

    a. pâté de foie gras   c. escargots

    b. caviare   d. potted shrimps   *p84 3.3*

42 The accompaniment offered separately with 'cocktail de crevettes' would be

    a. brown bread and butter

    b. segmented lemon

    c. Worcestershire sauce

    d. cayenne pepper and peppermill   *p86 3.3*

43 The waiter serves hot globe artichoke to a guest. Which of the following would be the correct accompaniment to offer?

    a. sauce mayonnaise

    b. sauce hollandaise

    c. sauce vinaigrette

    d. sauce raifort   *p86 3.3*

44 Oriental salt is a mixture of

    a. paprika and salt

    b. garlic salt and peppermill

    c. cayenne pepper and salt

    d. peppermill and salt   *p85 3.3*

45 You serve 'melon frappé' to a guest. The correct accompaniment should be

    a. brown bread and butter and a segment of lemon

    b. castor sugar and a segment of lemon

    c. ground ginger and a segment of lemon

    d. ground ginger and castor sugar   *p85 3.3*

Soup, egg and pasta dishes

46 The flavour of petit marmite is

    a. ham and lentil

    b. chicken and beef

    c. chicken and leek

    d. beef and onion   *p86 3.3*

47 With which of the following dishes would you *not*, offer grated parmesan cheese?

    a. minestroni

    b. soupe à l'oignon

    c. bortsch

    d. croûte au pot   *p87 3.3*

48 The only 'cream' soup traditionally served with croûtons offered separately is

    a. crème de céleri

    b. crème de légumes

    c. crème de champignons

    d. crème de tomates   *p86 3.3*

49 What would be the accompaniments to offer with Bortsch?

    a. sour cream, beetroot juice, bouchées filled with a duck liver pâté

    b. cayenne pepper, peppermill, segment of lemon

    c. peppermill, segment of lemon, brown bread and butter

    d. cheese straws, measure of sherry, brown bread and butter   *p87 3.3*

50 Which of the following sets of equipment would be used for the service of various egg dishes?

   a. petit marmite – ravier

   b. cocotte – sur le plat

   c. cocotte – ravier

   d. sur le plat – petit marmite   *p87 3.3*

51 Grated parmesan cheese is the accepted accompaniment to which of the following groups of dishes?

   a. spaghetti, moussaka, ravioli

   b. ravioli, paella, gnocchi Parisienne

   c. minestroni, bouillabaise, lasagne

   d. spaghetti, nouilles, gnocchi romaine   *p87 3.3*

52 Together with brown bread and butter and segments of lemon, the accompaniments for clear turtle soup are

   a. cheese straws, poached bone marrow

   b. grated parmesan cheese, poached bone marrow

   c. sherry, cheese straws

   d. sherry, grated parmesan cheese   *p87 3.3*

53 Thin slices of French bread dipped in oil and grilled are the correct accompaniments for the service of

   a. bouillabaisse

   b. tortue vraie

   c. consommé célestine

   d. Scotch broth   *p87 3.3*

54 Bouillabaisse may be described as a

   a. consommé thickened with egg yolks and cream

   b. Mediterranean fish stew

   c. duck flavoured consommé

   d. shellfish flavoured soup   *p87 3.3*

55   With which of the following soups would you offer poached
bone marrow?

    a. soupe à l'oignon

    b. bisque d'homard

    c. potage paysanne

    d. petit marmite   *p86 3.3*

Fish and meat dishes

56   The sauce offered with hareng grillé is

    a. sauce raifort

    b. sauce hollandaise

    c. beurre fondu

    d. sauce moutarde   *p88 3.3*

57   Cayenne pepper, peppermill, segment of lemon, brown bread
and butter are all accompaniments offered with

    a. blanchailles

    b. scampi frit

    c. saumon poché

    d. truite au bleu   *p88 3.3*

58   Together with brown bread and butter and segments of lemon
what other accompaniment would be offered with scampi frit?

    a. sauce tomate

    b. sauce tartare

    c. sauce mayonnaise

    d. sauce vinaigrette   *p88 3.3*

59   With which of the following dishes would you offer beurre
fondu as an accompaniment?

    a. sole Colbert   c. truite au bleu

    b. homard froid   d. moules marinière   *p89 3.3*

60 A guest orders filet de plie à l'Orly. Which of the following sauces would accompany this dish?

   a. sauce mousseline

   b. sauce suprême

   c. sauce remoulade

   d. sauce tomate   *p88 3.3*

61 Which of the following pairs of dishes has roast gravy, sage and onion stuffing and apple sauce as their traditional accompaniments?

   a. longe de porc rôti à l'Anglaise – oie rôti

   b. oie rôti – boeuf bouilli

   c. caneton rôti – aloyau de boeuf rôti à l'Anglaise

   d. tête de veau – longe de porc rôti à l'Anglaise
                                                              p89/90 3.3

62 The accompaniments to offer with gigot d'agneau rôti are

   a. caper sauce, savoury stuffing

   b. jus rôti, sauce menthe

   c. jus rôti, redcurrant jelly

   d. sauce à l'oignon, watercress   *p89 3.3*

63 Worcestershire sauce and pickled red cabbage would be offered with

   a. fricassé de volaille

   b. Lancashire hotpot

   c. salmis de gibier

   d. Irish stew   *p90 3.3*

64 Which of the following butters is normally served with grilled steaks?

   a. beurre d'ail   c. beurre maître d'hôtel

   b. beurre fondu   d. beurre d'anchois   *p90 3.3*

65 Sauce raifort would be offered with

    a. roast beef

    b. roast lamb

    c. roast game

    d. roast poultry   *p90 3.3*

Poultry, game and legumes

66 Which of the following 'stuffings' would you offer with poulet rôti à l'Anglaise?

    a. parsley and thyme

    b. chestnut

    c. sage and onion

    d. fines herbes   *p90 3.3*

67 Salade d'orange should be offered with

    a. perdreau

    b. canard

    c. oie

    d. dindonneau   *p90 3.3*

68 Which of the following pairs of accompaniments would a guest expect with dindonneau rôti à l'Anglaise?

    a. roast gravy – parsley and thyme stuffing

    b. bread sauce – lemon stuffing

    c. cranberry sauce – bacon rolls

    d. cranberry sauce – bread sauce   *p90 3.3*

69 Which of the following accompaniments would *not* be offered if you served Scotch Woodcock to a guest?

    a. Worcestershire sauce   c. cayenne pepper

    b. cruet   d. peppermill   *p98 3.4*

70 Redcurrant jelly should be offered with which of the following pairs of dishes?

a. lièvre – mouton bouilli

b. venison – selle de mouton rôti

c. épaule d'agneau rôti – lièvre

d. escalope de veau – venison   *p89/90 3.3*

71 A hot liver paste spread on a croûte is one of the accompaniments to

a. poulet rôti

b. canard sauvage

c. faisan rôti

d. poussin rôti   *p91 3.3*

72 With which of the following would you *not* offer French and English mustard?

a. entrecôte double

b. châteaubriand

c. porterhouse steak

d. steak tartare   *p90 3.3/p295 8.4*

73 Bombay duck may be described as

a. dried fillet of fish

b. speciality poultry dish

c. crisp highly seasoned pancake

d. game stew   *p89 3.3*

74 The accompaniments to offer with 'pomme au four' are

a. castor sugar, cream, mixed spice

b. peppermill, cayenne pepper, butter

c. peppermill, butter, segment of lemon

d. castor sugar, sauce Anglaise, ground cloves   *p91 3.3*

75 The following accompaniments have been offered with a roast game dish. Which is the odd one out?

  a. fried breadcrumbs, roast gravy

  b. liver paste on a croûte, watercress

  c. bread sauce, game chips

  d. redcurrant jelly, chestnut stuffing   *p91 3.3*

Covers

76 The plate to use in the service of hors-d'oeuvre is a

  a. sideplate

  b. fish plate

  c. joint plate

  d. salad crescent   *p83 3.3*

77 Which of the following spoons would be used when laying the cover for the service of demi-pamplemousse

  a. teaspoon

  b. preserve spoon

  c. sweet spoon

  d. grapefruit spoon   *p84 3.3*

78 Which of the following dishes requires a soup plate as part of the cover?

  a. petit marmite

  b. tortue vraie aux Xeres

  c. huîtres

  d. melon frappé   *p84 3.3*

79 Of the list of dishes shown below, which require a cold fish plate and fish knife and fork as part of the cover?

1	hors-d'oeuvre	a.	2–4–6–1
2	potted shrimps	b.	2–5–3–4
3	mousse de jambon	c.	1–2–4–5
4	anguille fumé	d.	1–3–5–6
5	saumon poché froid		
6	cocktail de crevettes		

p83–86 3.3

80 As well as a hot fish plate the cover for omelette served as a 'starter' course is

a. side knife and sweet fork

b. joint knife and fork

c. joint fork only

d. sweet spoon and fork   *p87 3.3*

81 The cover you have laid is a joint fork – sweet spoon – hot soup plate on an underplate. What dish are you serving?

a. lasagne

b. spaghetti

c. zabaglione

d. kari de boeuf   *p87 3.3*

82 A fingerbowl is used in the service of

a. potted shrimps

b. mais naturel

c. artichaut

d. escargots   *p86 3.3*

83 Which of the following items of equipment might be used in the service of Florida cocktail?

a.	ramekin	c.	hock glass
b.	demi-tasse	d.	coupe

p84 3.3

84   The cover for 'oeuf en cocotte à la crème' is

    a.   teaspoon

    b.   sweet spoon

    c.   sweet spoon and fork

    d.   side knife and sweet fork   *p87 3.3*

85   With which of the following main course dishes would you *not* use a steak knife as part of the cover?

    a.   entrecôte

    b.   porterhouse

    c.   steak tartare

    d.   mixed grill   *p90 3.3/p295 8.4*

Mixed

86   Cheese is made from

    a.   curds and whey

    b.   milk

    c.   butter

    d.   yoghurt   *p91 3.4*

87   Which of the following cheeses is most commonly used in cookery?

    a.   Cheshire

    b.   Derby

    c.   Leicester

    d.   Lancashire   *p91 3.4*

88   Cheddar is classified as a

    a.   hard cheese

    b.   semi-hard cheese

    c.   cream cheese

    d.   blue cheese   *p92 3.4*

89 Which of the following is the odd one out?

a. Gorgonzola

b. Roquefort

c. Double Gloucester

d. Stilton   *p93 3.4*

90 What is the country of origin of Caerphilly?

a. France

b. Denmark

c. England

d. Wales   *p93 3.4*

91 What is the cream cheese made in Normandy that is packed in light wooden circular boxes?

a. Camembert

b. Brie

c. Demi-sel

d. Carre de l'est   *p94 3.4*

92 The French blue cheese known as Roquefort is made from

a. cow's milk

b. ass's milk

c. ewe's milk

d. goat's milk   *p95 3.4*

93 When laying the cover for cheese the appropriate item of tableware required is a

a. joint knife and fork

b. cheese knife

c. joint knife

d. side knife   *p95 3.4*

94   When in season which of the following would be offered as an accompaniment with cheese?

   a. pineapple

   b. radish

   c. spring onion

   d. grapes   *p95 3.4*

95   What are the accompaniments for the service of dessert?

   a. salt, castor sugar

   b. cruet, castor sugar

   c. segments of lemon, cream

   d. sauce Anglaise, cream   *p96 3.4*

96   Which of the following liqueurs/spirits would you offer when serving fresh pineapple?

   a. rum

   b. brandy

   c. kirsch

   d. grand marnier   *p97 3.4*

97   The savoury 'Croûte Diane' contains

   a. ham

   b. chicken livers

   c. scrambled eggs

   d. soft roes   *p100 3.4*

98   A 'quiche lorraine' comes in the form of

   a. canapé

   b. bouchée

   c. soufflé

   d. flan   *p100 3.4*

99 Of the following cheeses which is most likely to be offered as an accompaniment to a dish by the food service operator?

a. Gruyère

b. Parmesan

c. Cheshire

d. Lancashire   *p86 3.3*

100 Horseradish sauce should be offered with which of the following groups of dishes?

1	anguille fumée	a.	1–2–3–4
2	contrefilet de boeuf rôti	b.	2–4–5–6
3	cuissot de porc rôti	c.	2–3–5–6
4	truite fumée	d.	1–2–4–5
5	chicken Maryland		
6	saumon fumée		*p84/89 3.3*

101 Which of the cheeses shown below might be served using a cheese scoop?

a. Gouda

b. Roquefort

c. Stilton

d. Camembert   *p96 3.4*

102 List four factors to note when storing cheese   *p92 3.4*

103 The cover for 'dessert' should contain two fingerbowls   *TRUE/FALSE*

If your answer is 'true' indicate briefly the use of each fingerbowl   *p96 3.4*

104 List nine items of equipment needed to prepare one cover for the service of 'dessert'   *p96 3.4*

105 A 'bouchée' may be described as a small puff pastry case   *TRUE/FALSE*   *p100 3.4*

106 Equate each cheese with its country of origin

a.	Edam	1	Italy	
b.	Brie	2	Holland	
c.	Wensleydale	3	England	
d.	Emmentaler	4	France	
e.	Gorgonzola	5	Switzerland	*p93/94 3.4*

107 What do the following menu garnishes denote?
1 Lyonnaise
2 Napolitaine
3 Polonaise
4 Veronique
5 au lard   *p64/67 3.1*

108 Which of the following would not come under the heading of 'potages' on an à la carte menu?

a. consommé

b. petit marmite

c. gnocchi

d. pilaff

e. bisque

f. bortsch

g. crème

h. moules   *p63 3.1/p81 3.2*

109 The menu term 'Florentine' denotes spinach   *TRUE/FALSE*
                                                 p64 3.1

110 The menu dish 'oeuf sur le plat' is served in the container in which it is cooked   *TRUE/FALSE*
                                                 p87 3.3

111 Name the two European cheeses commonly used in cookery   *p91 3.4*

112 Name two types of menu from which the guest may make his choice in a medium size hotel   *p69 3.1*

113 List four factors to consider when compiling a
menu   *p61 3.1*

114 Oysters are in season from April to September
TRUE/FALSE   *p76 3.2*

115 Match up the correct dish number with the correct
accompaniment

Dish	*Accompaniment*
1 Roast pork	Sauce hollandaise
2 Curry	Castor sugar
3 Smoked eel	Chilli vinegar
4 Tomato juice	Sauce tartare
5 Turtle soup	Grated parmesan cheese
6 Spaghetti	Worcestershire sauce
7 Oysters	Sherry
8 Deep fried fish	Mango chutney
9 Asparagus	Apple sauce
10 Grapefruit cocktail	Horseradish sauce

p82–91 3.3

Answers . . . .

1 b,   2 c,   3 d,   4 a,   5 b,   6 c,   7 d,   8 c,   9 b,   10 b,
11 d,   12 a,   13 b,   14 a,   15 b,   16 b,   17 c,   18 d,
19 a,   20 b,   21 b,   22 a,   23 b,   24 c,   25 d,   26 a,
27 c,   28 b,   29 d,   30 a,   31 d,   32 a,   33 b,   34 c,
35 d,   36 d,   37 c,   38 d,   39 a,   40 b,   41 c,   42 a,
43 b,   44 c,   45 d,   46 b,   47 c,   48 d,   49 a,   50 b,
51 d,   52 c,   53 a,   54 b,   55 d,   56 d,   57 a,   58 b,
59 c,   60 d,   61 a,   62 b,   63 d,   64 c,   65 a,   66 a,
67 b,   68 d,   69 a,   70 b,   71 c,   72 d,   73 a,   74 b,
75 d,   76 b,   77 d,   78 c,   79 c,   80 c,   81 b,   82 c,
83 d,   84 a,   85 c,   86 b,   87 d,   88 a,   89 c,   90 d,
91 a,   92 c,   93 d,   94 b,   95 a,   96 c,   97 b,   98 d,
99 b,   100 d,   101 c

102 Cool dark place; good air circulation; wrapped/boxed correctly; store away from foods which absorb flavours

103 True; for the guest to rinse fingers in lukewarm water, to rinse the required portion of grapes (cold water)

104 Fruit plate; fruit knife; fruit fork; spare napkin; fingerbowl for guest; fingerbowl to wash grapes; nutcrackers; grape scissors; spare sideplate

105 True

106 a 2; b 4; c 3; d 5; e 1

107 1 Onions; 2 Tomato and garlic flavoured sauce; 3 Fried breadcrumbs, chopped parsley, sieved hard boiled white and yolk of egg; 4 white wine sauce and grapes; 5 with bacon

108 c, d, h

109 True

110 True

111 Gruyère and Parmesan

112 À la carte/Table d'Hôte

113 Season; balance; availability of supplies; nutritional value; the occasion; colour

114 False

115 1 apple sauce; 2 mango chutney; 3 horseradish sauce; 4 Worcestershire sauce; 5 sherry; 6 grated parmesan cheese; 7 chilli vinegar; 8 sauce tartare; 9 sauce hollandaise; 10 castor sugar

4. BEVERAGES – NON-ALCOHOLIC AND ALCOHOLIC
(p101–168)

1   What is the capacity of a:

(i) *teacup*

a. 28.40cl (½ pint)

b. 9.47cl (⅙ pint)

c. 14.20cl (¼ pint)

d. 18.93cl (⅓ pint)

(ii) *demi-tasse*

a. ⅟₁₃ litre (⅙ pint)

b. ⅙ litre (⅓ pint)

c. ⅓ litre (⅔ pint)

d. ¼ litre (½ pint)

p104 4.1/p109 4.2

2   The container for the service of Russian tea is

a. a breakfast cup and saucer

b. a teacup and saucer

c. a glass tumbler in a silver holder

d. a Paris goblet on a doily and sideplate   *p105 4.1*

3   The flavouring agent used when making Turkish coffee is

a. cinnamon stick

b. vanilla pod

c. fig

d. lemon slices   *p115 4.2*

4   i. What quantity of dry tea is needed to make one gallon?

a. 2oz (56 grams)

b. 4oz (112 grams)

c. 6oz (168 grams)

d. 8oz (224 grams)   *p104 4.1*

ii. What quantity of ground coffee is needed to make one gallon?

a. 10oz (283 grams)

b. 1lb (454 grams)

c. 4oz (113 grams)

d. 8oz (227 grams)   *p109 4.2*

5   The term 'green tea' indicates

   a. a style of herb flavoured tea

   b. the colour of China tea

   c. the tea leaf has been fermented during the process of manufacture

   d. the tea leaf has not been fermented during the process of manufacture   *p104 4.1*

6   A demi-tasse would be used in the service of

   a. Turkish coffee

   b. consommé

   c. coffee

   d. China tea   *p109 4.2*

7   Which of the following may be classified as a tisane?

   a. darjeeling

   b. camomile

   c. orange pekoe

   d. earl grey   *p103 4.1*

8   China tea is correctly served in a

   a. teacup

   b. Paris goblet

   c. demi-tasse

   d. tumbler in a metal holder   *p105 4.1*

9   Another term used to describe the method of making 'Cona' coffee might be the

   a. drip method

   b. vacuum infusion method

   c. Rombouts method

   d. filter method   *p112 4.2*

10 An American equivalent to Café Hag is
   a. café cappuccino
   b. percolated coffee
   c. Sanka coffee
   d. Espresso coffee   *p115 4.2*

11 Russian tea is served with
   a. a sprig of mint
   b. double cream
   c. grated chocolate
   d. a slice of lemon   *p105 4.1*

12 Which is the odd one out?
   a. tisane
   b. Café Hag
   c. Sanka
   d. Rombouts   *p105 4.1/p113/114/115 4.1*

13 Which of the following 'coffees' is boiled in its production?
   a. café royale
   b. Turkish coffee
   c. Cona coffee
   d. instant coffee   *p115 4.2*

14 Bitter coffee may be caused by
   a. insufficient coffee
   b. water not reaching boiling point
   c. the infusion time being too long
   d. stale coffee being used   *p109 4.2*

15 The word tisane indicates

   a. a style of fruit syrup

   b. a decaffeinated coffee

   c. a hot malted milk drink

   d. an infusion of certain herbs   *p105 4.1*

16 Which of the following is not a mixed beer drink?

   a. shandy

   b. spritzer

   c. black velvet

   d. black and tan   *p166/167 4.13*

17 The substance used to clear and brighten beer is known as

   a. must

   b. stillions

   c. finings

   d. primings   *p165 4.13*

18 The process of 'racking' is carried out to

   a. encourage a slight secondary fermentation

   b. remove the sediment

   c. develop the condition of the beer

   d. attract sediment to the bottom of the cask   *p165 4.13*

19 The process of placing a porous or non-porous peg in the bung hole of a cask is known as

   a. racking

   b. fortifying

   c. tapping

   d. spiling   *p166/167 4.13*

20 The recognised storage temperature for bottled beer is

    a. 13–15°C

    b. 15–17°C

    c. 17–19°C

    d. 10–13°C   *p166 4.13*

21 Lager is a type of beer made by a

    a. distillation process

    b. malting process

    c. bottom fermentation process

    d. top fermentation process   *p165 4.13*

22 Which of the following is the odd one out?

    a. Malvern water

    b. tonic water

    c. dry ginger

    d. bitter lemon   *p118/119 4.4*

23 Perrier may be classified as a

    a. sulphurous water

    b. chalybeate water

    c. alkaline water

    d. aperient water   *p120 4.4*

24 A natural spring water from Germany would be

    a. Vichy

    b. Apollinaris

    c. Ashbourne

    d. Evian   *p118 4.4*

25 Which of the following groups of beverages are all flavoured with quinine?

    a. sherry, tonic water, Dubonnet

b. tonic water, Dubonnet, Campari

c. ginger ale, Campari, vermouth

d. pastis, vermouth, Perrier   *p118 4.4/p135 4.7*

26 Vermouth may be described as

   a. spirit distilled from grapes

   b. a sweetened and flavoured spirit

   c. a fortified wine

   d. an aromatised and fortified wine   *p134 4.7*

27 When serving 'gin and Italian', the Italian refers to

   a. sweet vermouth

   b. dry vermouth

   c. Angostura bitters

   d. fresh lemon juice   *p134 4.7*

28 The country of origin of Campari is

   a. France

   b. Italy

   c. Germany

   d. Greece   *p135 4.7*

29 Which of the following would not be classified as a pastis?

   a. Pernod

   b. Ouzo

   c. Manzanilla

   d. Ricard   *p136 4.7*

30 To make a pink gin one requires gin and

   a. dry vermouth

   b. Worcestershire sauce

   c. Fernet Branca

   d. Angostura bitters   *p130 4.6*

31 A bottle size for fruit juices is termed a

a. split

b. baby

c. nip

d. magnum   *p121 4.4*

32 The spirit found in café royale is

a. Tia Maria

b. rum

c. brandy

d. whisky   *p116 4.2*

33 A guest requests a glass of wine to accompany his fresh fruit salad and asks your advice. What would you suggest?

a. chilled sweet white wine

b. chilled dry madeira

c. medium dry red wine

d. not to have anything as it would not harmonise with the fruit flavours   *p150 4.10*

34 Grenadine may be classified as a

a. table water

b. aerated water

c. fruit juice

d. fruit syrup   *p121 4.4*

35 The predominant flavour of cassis is

a. cherry

b. blackcurrant

c. pomegranate

d. raspberry   *p121 4.4*

36   The prime cereal used in the production of beer is
 a. barley
 b. wheat
 c. rye
 d. maize   *p164 4.13*

37   The process of converting starch to sugar in the cereal is called
 a. osmosis
 b. finings
 c. maltings
 d. primings   *p165 4.13*

38   Hops are used in the production of beer because they
 a. add colour
 b. impart flavour
 c. give body to the end product
 d. act as a preservative   *p164 4.13*

39   When the malt has been crushed it is called
 a. powdered malt
 b. mash
 c. wort
 d. grist   *p165 4.13*

40   The two ingredients required to produce alcohol in the brewing
  process are
 a. sugar and yeast
 b. yeast and hops
 c. liquor and sugar
 d. hops and finings   *p165 4.13*

41 Which of the following items of equipment would be used in the making of cocktails?

   a. optics

   b. swizzle sticks

   c. hawthorn strainer

   d. coasters   *p128 4.6*

42 The bottle size known as a 'baby' contains

   a. half a pint (284ml)

   b. 7–8 fluid oz (213ml)

   c. 4 fluid oz (114ml)

   d. one pint (568ml)   *p121 4.4*

43 The term 'aperitif' denotes

   a. a type of fortified wine served prior to a meal

   b. a wine served to accompany a main meal

   c. a type of port, liqueur or brandy offered with coffee

   d. a range of drinks that may be served prior to a meal   *p134 4.7*

44 If a party of guests request dry sherry they will be served a

   a. Fino

   b. Amontillado

   c. Oloroso

   d. Noily Prat   *p134 4.7*

45 The size of measure normally used in the service of a vermouth is

   a. '6 out' optic

   b. '3 out' measure

   c. one-sixth of a gill

   d. '4 out' measure   *p134 4.7*

46 Which of the following is the odd one out?

    a. Chambery

    b. Noilly Prat

    c. Punt e Mes

    d. Cinzano dry   *p134 4.7*

47 Which of the following fortified wines should the sommelier *not* offer to a guest who has selected the menu dish 'choix de fromage' to follow his main course?

    a. madeira

    b. marsala

    c. port

    d. sherry   *p150 4.10*

48 The term 'spa' is recognised to denote

    a. where a natural spring water is to be found

    b. a French table water

    c. an English table water

    d. the mineral content of a natural spring water   *p120 4.4*

49 A firkin is a cask containing

    a. 18 gallons

    b. 36 gallons

    c. 4½ gallons

    d. 9 gallons   *p166 4.13*

50 Indicate the methods of making coffee indicated by the following

    a. Cona

    b. Cafetière

    c. Rombouts

    d. Still set   *p111/112/113/114 4.2*

51 Espresso coffee is traditionally served in a small glass
cup   *TRUE/FALSE*   *p114 4.2*

52 When serving 'speciality coffees' – that is with cream – it is
better to use double cream because it floats more easily due to a
higher fat content   *TRUE/FALSE*   *p116 4.2*

53 List four factors which indicate the correct storage of tea or
coffee   *p104 4.1/p108 4.2*

54 Name three methods of serving tea where slices of lemon are
offered as a garnish   *p105 4.1*

55 How many guests at a buffet style operation could you serve
from a three-gallon urn of black coffee if you offered them all
tea-cups of coffee made up of half black coffee and half hot
milk?   *p109 4.2*

56 List the order in which the ingredients should be placed in the
Paris goblet to make an Irish coffee.   *p117 4.2*

57 List six of the factors which help to determine good cellar
management   *p167 4.13*

58 List the five categories into which dispense bar beverages may be
classified   *p118 4.4*

59 mineral waters are usually classified according to their chemical
properties   *TRUE/FALSE*   *p120 4.4*

60 On delivery of cask beer to your cellar it should be placed
immediately upon the stillions   *TRUE/FALSE*
                                               p167 4.13

61 List the quantities contained in the following draught beer casks

a. pin

b. barrel

c. firkin

d. keg   *p166 4.13*

62 Indicate four advantages of selling 'canned beer' in your
    establishment   *p166 4.13*

63 Gomme is a white sugar syrup that may be used as a base for
    certain cocktails   *TRUE/FALSE*   *p121 4.4*

64 Name four English mineral waters   *p119/120 4.4*

65 Tasting may be said to be an analysis of wine by the senses.
    Which senses are involved?   *p149 4.4*

66 A draught beer cask containing 18 gallons is known as a
    hogshead   *TRUE/FALSE*   *p166 4.13*

67 In the production of beer what ingredients are put together to
    make that mixture known as 'wort'?   *p165 4.13*

68 Wines to accompany fish dishes are normally

    a. white and sweet

    b. white and dry

    c. rosé and light red

    d. sparkling only   *p151 4.10*

69 A red wine suitable to accompany both lamb and beef might be

    a. Meursault

    b. Sancerre

    c. Fleurie

    d. Château Olivier   *p151/152 4.10*

70 Which of the following wines would be most suitable to
    complement 'dessert'?

    a. Barsac

    b. Chablis

    c. Muscadet

    d. Liebfraumilch   *p152 4.10*

71 It is generally recognised that Stilton harmonises best with

   a. Chianti Classico

   b. Nuits St Georges

   c. Asti Spumanti

   d. port   *p152/153 4.10*

72 Liqueurs may be defined as

   a. aromatised and fortified wines

   b. liquors produced from an alcoholic wash

   c. sweetened and flavoured spirits

   d. fortified wines   *p155 4.11*

73 Which of the following would *not* be classified as a 'Pastis'?

   a. Ricard

   b. Ouzo

   c. Lillet

   d. Pernod   *p136 4.7*

74 Champagne is produced in vineyards having mainly a

   a. chalk soil

   b. gravel or pebble soil

   c. limestone soil

   d. slate soil   *p139 4.8*

75 The main grape species producing fine white Burgundy and
    Californian wine is

   a. Palomino

   b. Chardonnay

   c. Pinot Noir

   d. Gamay   *p140 4.8*

76 The term indicating the 'grape harvest' that takes place in the Northern hemisphere, in late September or early October is

  a. Vigneron

  b. Phylloxera

  c. Vendage

  d. Kabinett   *p141 4.8*

77 The colour in red wine comes from

  a. the flesh of the grape itself

  b. the addition of cochineal

  c. the tannins found in the stalk of the grape

  d. the skin of the grape   *p142 4.8*

78 The champagne label term meaning 'dry' is

  a. demi-sec

  b. doux

  c. brut

  d. sec   *p143 4.8*

79 Within the EEC the term indicating 'fortified wines' is

  a. pétillant

  b. vins de liqueur

  c. auslese

  d. sercial   *p144 4.8*

80 The second quality wines of France produced from specific vineyards and districts are shown by the label term

  a. VDQS

  b. AOC

  c. QBA

  d. DOC   *p144 4.8*

81 The process of producing 'spirits' is known as

    a. distillation

    b. fermentation

    c. malting

    d. maturing   *p156 4.12*

82 'Heads', 'Hearts' and 'Tails' are all terms relating to

    a. fortified liquors

    b. liqueurs

    c. wines

    d. spirits   *p157 4.12*

83 The principle flavouring agents used in the production of gin are

    a. juniper berry and coriander seed

    b. fuggles and goldings

    c. malted cereals

    d. vanilla pods   *p158 4.12*

84 The spirit that is made up from the fermented by-products of sugar cane is

    a. whisky

    b. vodka

    c. rum

    d. brandy   *p158 4.12*

85 The colour of 'dark rum' is obtained through the addition of

    a. brown sugar

    b. molasses

    c. yeast extracts

    d. caramel   *p159 4.12*

86   Dimple Haig, Johnny Walker Black Label, Glenlivet, and Bell's
are all well known brand names of

   a. whisky

   b. gin

   c. vodka

   d. brandy   *p160 4.12*

87   The predominant cereal used in the production of Canadian
whisky is

   a. wheat

   b. rye

   c. maize

   d. barley   *p161 4.12*

88   'Jack Daniels' is a well known brand name of

   a. Irish whiskey

   b. American whiskey

   c. Canadian whisky

   d. Scotch whisky   *p161 4.12*

89   'Grande Champagne' is a region in the area of

   a. Bordeaux

   b. Champagne

   c. Cognac

   d. Armagnac   *p162 4.12*

90   The colourless liqueur produced from cherries is

   a. Kirsch

   b. Grappa

   c. Slivovitz

   d. Vodka   *p163 4.12*

91 The substance used to clear and brighten beer is

    a. grist

    b. finings

    c. primings

    d. wort   *p165 4.13*

92 The process of running off the beer from one cask to another to leave the sediment behind is called

    a. racking

    b. pitching

    c. malting

    d. sparging   *p165 4.13*

93 Bottled beer should be stored at a constant temperature of

    a. 8–10°C

    b. 10–12°C

    c. 13–15°C

    d. 15–18°C   *p166 4.13*

94 The process that takes place in the cellar to reduce the pressure in a cask is known as

    a. decanting

    b. maturing

    c. tapping

    d. spiling   *p167 4.13*

95 Cider is an alcoholic beverage obtained through the fermentation of

    a. apple juice

    b. pear juice

    c. grape juice

    d. must   *p167 4.14*

96 'Bloom' is a term used in connection with wine production to describe

   a. the flower on the vine

   b. the yeast on the grape skins

   c. the bouquet of the wine

   d. a type of vine pruning method   *p152 4.8*

97 Vitis vinifera is

   a. a type of yeast

   b. a method of training vines

   c. a species of vine

   d. a vineyard owned by a co-operative   *p139 4.8*

Answers . . . .

1 (i) d (ii) a, 2 c, 3 b, 4 (i) a (ii) a, 5 d, 6 c, 7 b, 8 a,
9 b, 10 c, 11 d, 12 a, 13 b, 14 c, 15 d, 16 b,
17 c, 18 b, 19 d, 20 a, 21 c, 22 a, 23 c, 24 b,
25 b, 26 d, 27 a, 28 b, 29 c, 30 d, 31 b, 32 c,
33 a, 34 d, 35 b, 36 a, 37 c, 38 b, 39 d, 40 a,
41 c, 42 c, 43 d, 44 a, 45 b, 46 c, 47 d, 48 a, 49 d

50 vacuum infusion; infusion; individual filter; filter

51 True

52 True

53 Dry clean covered container; well ventilated stillroom; no excess moisture; not stored near any strong smelling food items; air tight container for ground coffee

54 China tea; Russian tea; iced tea

55 144

56 1 sugar, 2 very hot black coffee, 3 Irish whiskey, 4 double cream

57 ventilation; cleanliness; even temperature; correct storage; regular cleaning of equipment; adequate stock

58 Aerated waters;   natural spring/mineral water;   squashes;
    juices;   syrups

59 True

60 True

61 a. 4½ gallons;   b. 36 gallons;   c. 9 gallons;   d. 10 gallons

62 Storage;   no breakages;   long shelf life;   minimum risk of
    deterioration

63 True

64 Ashbourne;   Buxton;   Malvern;   Cheltenham;   Harrogate

65 Sight;   smell;   taste

66 False

67 Barley;   liquor;   hops and sugar

68 b,	69 c,	70 a,	71 d,	72 c,	73 c,	74 a,	75 b,
76 c,	77 d,	78 c,	79 b,	80 a,	81 a,	82 d,	83 a,
84 c,	85 d,	86 a,	87 b,	88 b,	89 c,	90 a,	91 b,
92 a,	93 c,	94 d,	95 a,	96 b,	97 c		

5. THE FOOD AND BEVERAGE SERVICE SEQUENCE
(p169–243)

1   The purpose of a good visual display of dishes in cafeteria service and on buffets is to

   a. enable the chef to sell leftovers

   b. promote more atmosphere with a colourful display

   c. keep replenishment of the counter or buffet to a minimum

   d. act as a selling aid and encourage guests to purchase   *p199 5.4*

2   The 'centre plate' used in an à la carte cover is a

   a. sideplate

   b. fish plate

   c. joint plate

   d. sweet plate   *p194/195 5.4*

3   How many items of cutlery and flatware make up a Table d'Hôte cover?

   a. 6   c. 8

   b. 5   d. 3   *p194 5.4*

4   Where is the wine glass positioned in relation to the cover laid?

   a. top left hand corner of the cover

   b. head of the cover

   c. right hand side of the cover

   d. top right hand corner of the cover   *p195/196 5.4*

5   Which of the following items is not normally laid on the table as part of the mise en place?

   a. chilled butter portions   c. floral decor

   b. Paris goblet   d. cruet   *p198 5.4*

6   The process of 'crumbing down' normally takes place?

  a. after each course

  b. after the main course

  c. at the conclusion of the meal but before the bill is presented

  d. immediately prior to the service of coffee

  p174 5.1/p204 5.5

7   What is the main reason why the more simple napkin folds are used in every day service?

  a. they are appreciated more by the customers

  b. less time is required to fold them

  c. the question of hygiene

  d. because they unfold more easily   *p193 5.4*

8   Which of the following is the odd one out?

  a. cone

  b. cockscombe

  c. bishop's mitre

  d. Cona   *p112 4.2/p193 5.4*

9   When laying a Table d'Hôte cover the first item to be laid would be the

  a. napkin

  b. sideplate

  c. meat knife and fork

  d. soup spoon   *p196 5.4*

10 Badged china should be laid with the crest

  a. nearest to the guest

  b. at the head of the cover

  c. to either the left or right of the cover

  d. in any position   *p196 5.4*

11   A table with four covers laid has only three guests seated. The spare cover should have been

    a. removed prior to the guests being seated

    b. left as part of the next relay

    c. removed immediately the guests are seated

    d. removed once the 'starters' have been served   *p205 5.5*

12   'Plated' food is normally served from

    a. either side of the guest

    b. the right

    c. the host and then straight around the table

    d. the left   *p213 5.7*

13   The order for a bottle of wine will be taken by the sommelier

    a. before the food order has been taken

    b. once the food order has been taken

    c. immediately before the main course is served

    d. on request from the host   *p220 5.8*

14   When taking a booking the essential information required would be

    a. name, address, number of covers, date

    b. number of covers, time, price, name

    c. date, name , number of covers, time

    d. menu, name, date, price   *p184 5.3*

15   When serving food and drink to a party of four guests, the person to be served last would be the

    a. eldest female

    b. youngest male

    c. eldest male

    d. host   *p221 5.8*

16 When using the triplicate checking system the information to be completed in the four corners of the food check will be

a. time of arrival, number of covers, name of host, signature

b. signature of supervisor, table number, number of covers, date

c. table number, number of covers, date, signature of waiter

d. table number, number of covers, date, price of meal   *p206 5.6*

17 What is the French term used as a heading at the top of the 'sweet' and 'coffee' checks?

a. saignant

b. tournant

c. supplement

d. suivant   *p207 5.6*

18 The top copy of the food check goes to the

a. aboyeur

b. cashier

c. waiter

d. debarrasseur   *p206 5.6*

19 When an extra portion of food is required what is the French term that is written at the top of the food check?

a. baveuse

b. supplement

c. retour

d. en place   *p207 5.6*

20   When the triplicate checking system is in use and the cashier makes out the guests bill, how many copies of the latter are there?

a. four

b. one

c. two

d. three   *p239 5.11*

21   The correct/traditional method of presenting a guest's bill is on a doily on a sideplate, with the bill

a. unfolded and facing upwards

b. unfolded and face downwards

c. folded in half

d. folded in half and the corner over the total turned up
                                                                              p239 5.11

22   Should a guest complain about the meal being served, the food service operator must

a. rectify as far as is possible and then refer to the chef de cuisine

b. restify as far as is possible and then refer to the aboyeur

c. rectify as far as is possible and then refer to his/her immediate superior

d. report the complaint on completion of the service, and before going off-duty   *p178 5.2*

23   If a party of four ladies arrived at the entrance of your coffee shop should the supervisor

a. allow them to select their own table

b. greet them and indicate which table they are to sit at

c. call a waiter over to show them to their table

d. greet them and ask them to follow him/her to the appropriate table   *p178 5.2*

24 A 'family' have booked for 'dinner' in your restaurant. Who should be seated first on arrival at the table?

a. the eldest male

b. the eldest female

c. the host

d. the youngest female   *p178 5.2*

25 If a guest requests a dish to be changed for any reason, the food service operator must

a. write out a food check headed 'suivant'

b. write out a 'retour' and 'en place' food check

c. write out a food check headed 'supplement'

d. write out an 'accident' check   *p207/208 5.6*

26 A waiter finds a purse under a chair recently vacated by a regular guest, they should

a. keep the purse until the end of service and then return it to the Head Waiter for safe keeping

b. keep the purse until the guests next visit to the restaurant

c. check if the guest has left the vicinity of the restaurant and if so immediately hand the purse to her superior

d. place the contents of the purse in the tronc   *p181 5.2*

27 Before any lost property is returned, which of the following should be requested of the recipient?

a. proof of identity

b. description of article to be returned

c. signature and address

d. all of the above   *p181 5.2*

28 As the supervisor, you suspect that a prospective guest asking for a table has had too much to drink. You should

a. refuse a table even though there is one available

b. refuse a table only if there are none available

   c. offer the guest a table but refuse to serve any alcoholic
beverage

   d. call security for assistance in case of any
trouble   *p183 5.2*

29 A male guest arrives at your dining area wearing no jacket. His
dress therefore does not meet the standards laid down by your
establishment. You should

   a. refuse him a table even though previously booked

   b. warn him that this must not happen again and then seat his
party

   c. offer him a jacket to wear for the period of time he is dining

   d. immediately call management to determine what action you
should take   *p183 5.2*

30 The top copy of the wine check goes to the

   a. dispense bar

   b. cashier

   c. control department

   d. cellar   *p213 5.2*

31 If you serve a resident and he wishes to sign the 'check' for
services received, which of the following items of information
change when writing out the drink checks?

   a. date

   b. signature

   c. table number

   d. number of covers   *p212 5.6*

32 The correct distribution of food checks when using the triplicate
checking system is

   a. bottom to kitchen, top to cashier, flimsy retained by waiter

   b. top to kitchen, bottom copy to cashier, flimsy to waitress

   c. top to kitchen, bottom to headwaiter, flimsy to cashier

d. top to cash desk, flimsy to kitchen, duplicate retained by
waiter   *p206/207 5.6*

33 If the food service operator has spilt a little sauce down the front
of a guest, they should apologise and

a. hand a clean damp cloth to the guest

b. say it will not happen again

c. report the incident immediately to the head waiter

d. wipe the sauce away and offer to pay any dry cleaning
expenses   *p179 5.2*

34 A table d'hôte food check differs from an à la carte food check
in that

a. the duplicate copy goes to the kitchen

b. all the dishes ordered are individually priced

c. the set charge for the meal is shown on the food check

d. the food check acts as the bill   *p206 5.6*

35 A triplicate checking system would normally be used in

a. a first-class restaurant

b. a department store

c. a coffee shop

d. popular price restaurants   *p206 5.6*

36 The main course meat/fish dish when served on to the hot joint
plate should be positioned at

a. 3 o'clock

b. 6 o'clock

c. 9 o'clock

d. 12 o'clock   *p214 5.7*

37 When silver serving potato and vegetable from a double vegetable dish which of the following equipment does the server need?

   a. underflat, service cloth, sets of service spoon and fork for each different item being served

   b. underflat, service cloth, only one set of service spoons and forks

   c. service cloth, set of service spoons and forks for each different item being served

   d. underflat with napkin on it, service cloth, sets of service spoon and fork for each different item being served   *p215 5.7*

38 The most efficient method of serving an omelette is to use

   a. two service forks

   b. two fish knives

   c. a slice

   d. a service spoon and fork   *p216 5.7*

39 Table water should be served at

   a. 18–19°C

   b. 13–16°C

   c. 10–13°C

   d. 7–10°C   *p230 5.9*

40 Of the following pairs of glasses which is the most suitable for the service of a natural spring water?

   a. 6⅔ fl. oz Paris goblet, Slim Jim

   b. Wellington, Pilsner

   c. tulip, highball

   d. Worthington, '3 out' Elgin   *p230 5.9*

41 With which of the following fruit juices should a waiter offer Worcestershire sauce as an accompaniment?

   a. jus de pamplemousse   c. jus de tomate

   b. jus d'orange   d. jus d'ananas   *p231 5.9*

42 Which of the following flavouring agents is often found in French coffee?

a. vanilla

b. figs

c. chicory

d. caffein   p228 5.9

43 Which of the following is a glass unsuitable for the service of bottled beer?

a. Slim Jim

b. Pilsner

c. Worthington

d. Wellington   p224 5.8

44 Grease on a glass into which beer is being poured may cause it to

a. go cloudy

b. go flat

c. lose its flavour

d. become darker in colour   p224 5.8

45 Which of the following terms denotes a liqueur served on crushed ice?

a. claro

b. chambre

c. frappé

d. must   p225 5.8

46 White table wines are normally served at the following temperatures

a. 13–15°C

b. 10–12°C

c. 7–9°C

d. 15–17°C   p223 5.8

47 Which of the following items of equipment is required to assist in opening a bottle of champagne?

a. waiter's friend

b. serviette

c. cork extractor

d. wine basket   *p222 5.8*

48 Which of the following is *not* recognised as a type of buffet service operation?

a. spoon and fork

b. knife and fork

c. fork

d. finger   *p198 5.4*

49 The layout of the service counter in cafeteria service is most important. Which order of layout would you consider to be correct?

a. tableware – cold items – hot items – beverages – cashier

b. menu – cold items – hot items – beverages – cashier

c. menu – beverages – cold items – hot items – cashier

d. hot items – cold items – beverages – cashier – tableware   *p199 5.4*

50 In cafeteria service the menu will normally be

a. offered to guests by the waiter

b. displayed on each table

c. displayed near the entrance of the food service area

d. shown to customers on request   *p199 5.4*

51 What is the definition of the term 'mise-en-place'?

a. pre-service preparation

b. the team of restaurant staff

c. a type of restaurant menu

d. the degree of cooking for a steak   *p185 5.4*

52 In cafeteria service good presentation and display of food is essential

   a. to give a good visual effect to the guest

   b. to promote atmosphere in the food service area

   c. to ensure good portion control

   d. to maximise sales   *p199 5.4*

53 One definition of the word 'covers' in relation to the restaurant is

   a. the guests attending a function

   b. the slip cloche used for covering a slightly soiled tablecloth

   c. the cloth used to cover a flat containing a number of portions of meat

   d. any type of tray cloth that may be placed on breakfast trays   *p194 5.4*

54 Which of the following would you consider most important when dealing with an emergency?

   a. profuse apologies to the guest

   b. a sense of urgency

   c. to spend time looking for your superior to inform him of the action you will take

   d. to finish serving the other tables on your station before taking any action   *p178 5.2*

55 A guest suddenly feels unwell and has to return home immediately, in a taxi called for by the establishment. The subsequent action taken should be to

   a. charge for the full meal ordered and the taxi fare

   b. charge proportionately for that part of the meal consumed only

   c. charge only for the taxi fare

   d. follow company policy and charge accordingly   *p182 5.2*

56 When writing the order for a bottle of wine the sommelier will

   a. write the full name of the wine

   b. write the name of the wine in abbreviated form

   c. write the name of the wine and the year

   d. write the bin number   *p213 5.6*

57 When 'chance' guests order alcoholic beverages to accompany their meal the four items of information to be completed in each corner of the wine check are

   a. number of covers, date, signature, room no.

   b. table no., number of covers, date, signature

   c. table no., date, signature, total cash price of order

   d. table no., date, total cash price of order, number of covers   *p212 5.6*

58 List six items required by the chef de salle for the efficient service of a fruit squash in the lounge   *p231 5.9*

59 The waiter asks the guest if she would like 'black' or 'white' coffee. Is this correct? if not, why?   *p288 5.9*

60 List the three terms which indicate the component parts of a cigar   *p225 5.8*

61 At what temperature should cigars be stored?   *p226 5.8*

62 What are the advantages of using a service salver when clearing side plates and side knives?   *p236 5.10*

63 What items of equipment do you require to 'crumb down'?   *p237 5.10*

64 From which side of the cover should you crumb down and why?   *p237 5.10*

65 What is the purpose of crumbing down?   *p237 5.10*

66 After crumbing down on which sides of the place setting would the sweet spoon and fork be placed?   *p237 5.10*

67 What side of the cover do you clear 'dirties'
    from?   *p232 5.10*

68 What side of the cover do you clear sideplates from and
    why?   *p203 5.5*

69 Indicate five 'actions' that should happen at the table
    immediately the guests have been seated   *p203 5.5*

70 Give two reasons why it is important to carry out the correct
    clearing techniques   *p232 5.10*

71 Draw a diagram of an à la carte cover and list the items of
    equipment used   *p194/195 5.4*

72 List the order of laying equipment to complete one table d'hôte
    cover   *p196 5.4*

73 What do the letters N/C stand for when written on an accident
    check?   *p207/208 5.6*

74 In duplicate checking what is the purpose of the following?

    a. a supplementary check pad

    b. a waiter's account slip   *p211 5.6*

75 List four points to consider prior to laying a
    tablecloth   *p192 5.4*

76 Indicate three reasons why 'simple' napkin folds are mainly used
    in a food service area   *p193 5.4*

77 Name six napkin folds   *p193 5.4*

78 What napkin fold might be used to hold both the menu and a
    place card?   *p193 5.4*

79 Name two methods of carrying glasses and indicate when each
    method would be used   *p174 5.1*

80 What method of cleaning glasses would you use during the
    mise-en-place?   *p197 5.4*

81 As the food service operator, at what stage during the service of a meal would you consider that the ashtrays should be changed?   p237 5.10

82 The full silver service approach in the service of a meal will be most efficiently carried out using which items of tableware?   p170 5.1

83 The ends of an omelette should be trimmed immediately before serving   *TRUE/FALSE*   p216 5.7

84 Name four types of pre-portioned food items that may be used in a self-service counter operation   p200 5.4

85 In full silver service the main dish should be presented to the guest before serving   *TRUE/FALSE*   p214 5.7

86 List four uses of a service salver   p172 5.1

87 Portion control is important in relation to all forms of food service. List six items of equipment which would ensure standardisation in portion control   p200 5.4

88 State four reasons why staff should come on duty a few minutes early   p203 5.5

89 What is the reason for putting the coffee service down from the right and placing it on the right-hand side of the cover?   p228 5.9

90 Name a napkin fold in which Melba toast may be presented on the table?   p193 5.4

91 A report should be made of every accident/incident however trivial   *TRUE/FALSE*   p183 5.2

92 In certain forms of duplicate checking when writing out a guest's order a different perforated slip would be used for each course   *TRUE/FALSE*   p210 5.6

93 From which side of the cover will the coffee service be placed on the table?   p228 5.9

94 Coffee is always served from the left   *TRUE/FALSE*

p228 5.9

95 What is the correct order of ingredients into the demi-tasse when silver serving coffee?   *p228/229 5.9*

96 In the restaurant during the meal service all glassware should be carried on a service salver   *TRUE/FALSE*   *p172 5.1*

97 List any six tasks that might be included in the restaurant mise-en-place   *5.4*

98 The station head waiter will normally take the food order through which member of a party of guests?   *p203 5.5*

99 List four factors that should be considered when writing a food check?   *p206 5.6*

100 Indicate briefly the purpose of the terms 'retour' and 'en place' sometimes seen on a food check   *p207/208 5.6*

101 In counter service the tableware stands are normally positioned after the cashier   *TRUE/FALSE*   *p199 5.4*

102 What type of checking system would be used in a first-class or luxury restaurant?   *p206 5.6*

103 Champagne or any sparkling wine would normally be served in what type of wine glass?   *p222/223 5.8*

104 The host complains because the sommelier has served the red wine ordered frappé. Who was correct and why?   *p222/223 5.2*

105 A client who appears to be seriously ill in your dining area should be moved immediately to a 'sick room' to await the arrival of a doctor or someone qualified in first aid to make a diagnosis   *TRUE/FALSE*   *p182 5.2*

106 The contents of a wallet found by the commis de rang should, if the owner cannot be immediately located, be listed. This list should be signed by which two people?   *p181 5.2*

107 List the main points to be noted in an incident book

p183 5.2

108 State two reasons why it is necessary to write out a 'retour'/'en place' food check

p207 5.6

109 Where an à la carte cover has been laid the cutlery and flatware normally required by the guest, in relation to the food order given, will be laid course by course   *TRUE/FALSE*

p197 5.4

110 What is a service plate? Indicate two uses of this piece of equipment

p173 5.1

111 Indicate four factors which help determine that a tablecloth has been laid correctly.

p192 5.4

112 Alcoholic beverages are always served from the left
TRUE/FALSE

p203 5.5

113 Indicate three reasons why an efficient system of control should be maintained by the sommeliers and the dispense barstaff

p212 5.6

114 What is the function of a bin number as shown on a wine list?

p213 5.6

115 Below is a '15 minute' general knowledge exercise indicating some of the detailed information a food service operator should be aware of. What can you achieve?

(A) Revision test

Explain the meaning of the following menu terms
  1 entrecôte grillé
  2 foie de veau
State the accompaniments to be served with
  3 saumon fumé
  4 longe de porc rôti
What is the 'cover' a waiter should lay for the following dishes?
  5 consommé royale
  6 kari de boeuf madras

Miscellaneous:
7 What are the two main types of menu?
8 State three different sizes of tablecloth
9 Where does the top copy of the wine check go?
10 List three different ways in which coffee may be served

(B) Right or wrong?

Read each statement carefully and then answer it using the word
RIGHT or WRONG
1 Oil and vinegar are the accompaniments for hors d'oeuvres
2 A waiter should position himself between the legs of a table in
order to lay a tablecloth correctly
3 A sweet spoon and fork and a hot fish plate are the cover
required for spaghetti
4 Gaelic coffee has rum added to it
5 The team of staff working together in a dining room is called
a brigade

(C) True or false?

Read each statement carefully and then answer it using the
words TRUE or FALSE
1 Castor sugar is an accompaniment with cream cheese
2 The waiter in charge of a station is the débarrasseur
3 A soup spoon is laid as part of the cover when a consommé is
to be served
4 Lager is a beer which should be served chilled
5 Burnishing is a method of cleaning silver

Answers . . . .

1 d, 2 b, 3 c, 4 d, 5 a, 6 b, 7 c, 8 d, 9 a, 10 b,
11 c, 12 b, 13 b, 14 c, 15 d, 16 c, 17 d, 18 a,
19 b, 20 c, 21 d, 22 c, 23 d, 24 b, 25 b, 26 c,
27 d, 28 a, 29 c, 30 a, 31 c, 32 b, 33 a, 34 c,
35 a, 36 b, 37 d, 38 c, 39 d, 40 a, 41 c, 42 c,
43 a, 44 b, 45 c, 46 b, 47 b, 48 a, 49 b, 50 c,
51 a, 52 d, 53 a, 54 b, 55 d, 56 d, 57 b

58 Tumbler/short stemmed beer glass; straws; jug of iced water;
small ice-bucket and tongs; soda syphon; coaster

59 No – there is no such things as 'white' coffee – it should be
'coffee with milk or cream'

60 Filler; binder; wrapper

61 15–18°C; between 55–60% humidity

62 A larger 'working surface' is available on which to clear the dirty sideknives and any debris

63 Service plate and a service/waiters cloth

64 Both sides of each 'cover' – so that you do not ever stretch across the front of a guest

65 To remove any 'crumbs' or 'debris' left on the tablecloth

66 Sweet spoon on the right and sweet fork on the left of the place setting

67 Right

68 Left – because they are on the left of the 'cover' and you do not then stretch across the front of the guest

69 Assist in seating guests; unfold napkins; wine glass up the correct way; butter placed upon the table; rolls or Melba toast offered; menu presented

70 Speed and efficiency around the table; avoids the possibility of accidents; minimum inconvenience to the guests

71 Fish plate; napkin; fish knife; fish fork; sideplate; sideknife; Paris goblet

72 Napkin; joint knife; fish knife; soup spoon; joint fork; fish fork; sweet fork; sweet spoon; sideplate; sideknife; Paris goblet

73 No charge

74 a. extra items ordered; b. food service operators record of cash taken

75 Table in its correct position, table top clean, table is level and does not wobble, check for the correct size of tablecloth

76 Appearance; hygiene; time available

77 Cone; bishops mitre; rose; Prince of Wales feathers; cockscombe; triple wave

78 Triple wave

79 Hand – during pre-preparation; service salver – during the meal 'service'

80 By hand

81 At any stage should you feel it necessary

82 Service spoons and forks

83 True

84 Butter; sugar; cream; milk; cheese; biscuits

85 True

86 Carrying clean glasses; removing clean cutlery and flatware from the table; for placing clean cutlery and flatware on the table; for placing coffee services on the table; as an underflat when silver serving vegetables

87 Scoops; ladles; bowls; milk dispenser; cold beverage dispensers; measuring jugs

88 Check sideboards, check tables, check menu, check personal presentation

89 Because the 'coffee' will be served from the right hand side of the guest

90 Rose

91 True

92 True

93 Right

94 False

95 Coffee sugar; black coffee; milk/cream

96 True

97 Accompaniments; hotplate; stillroom; sideboards; linen; housekeeping duties

98 The host

99 Legibility; abbreviations; prices of dishes/meal; correct format

100 Retour – a dish returned to the kitchen; en place – the dish taking its place

101 True

102 Triplicate

103 Flute/tulip

104 The host is correct – red wine is served at 18/19°C – unless young red wines which may be served slightly chilled

105 False

106 Supervisor and commis de rang

107 Place; date; time; nature of incident; individual reports; action taken; name, address, phone numbers of the persons involved

108 A wrong dish has been ordered; something wrong with a 'food item' and it has to be replaced

109 True

110 Joint plate with a napkin upon it; crumbing down/placing clean cutlery and flatware upon the table

111 Corners of the cloth cover the legs of the table; overlap even around the table; main creases of the tablecloths should all run in the same direction in the room; where two tablecloths have been used on one table then the 'overlap' should face away from the entrance to the room

112 False

113 To ensure the correct drinks are served at the right table; the service rendered is charged to the correct bill; to ensure a record is kept of all 'drinks' issued from the dispense bar

114 The bin number acts as an aid to the bar staff/cellarman in finding a specific wine

115 (a) 1 Grilled entrecôte steak (steak from the sirloin of beef)
2 Calves liver 3 Cayenne pepper, peppermill, segment of lemon, brown bread and butter 4 Apple suace, roast gravy, sage and onion stuffing 5 Consommé cup on a consommé saucer on a fish plate, sweet spoon 6 Joint knife and fork and a sweet spoon 7 À la carte, table d'hôte 8 54″ × 54″, 72″ × 72″, 54″ × 72″, 6ft × 12ft 9 Dispense bar 10 Cafetière, Espresso, Silver service, Cona

(b) 1 Right 2 Right 3 Wrong 4 Wrong 5 Right

(c) 1 True 2 False 3 False 4 True 5 True

6. THE SERVICE OF BREAKFAST AND AFTERNOON TEA
(p244–257)

1 A guest ordering a Full English Breakfast in your restaurant will expect to receive

    a. coffee, croissants, preserves, butter and a fruit juice

    b. a limited choice menu with a cooked main course to be silver served

    c. a set three course meal with tea as the beverage

    d. a wide selection from which to choose, and with a cooked main course that will be 'plate served'   *p246/252 6.1*

2 The term 'café complet' means

    a. coffee only

    b. a continental breakfast with coffee

    c. a full English breakfast with coffee

    d. coffee only, but silver served at the table   *p245 6.1*

3 Which of the following groups of fish dishes might be most suitable for a breakfast menu?

    a. aiglefin fumé, merlan

    b. sole de Douvre, hareng

    c. kippers, kedgeree

    d. kedgeree, anguille fumée   *p246 6.1*

4 The checking system usually used for the service of full afternoon tea is

    a. duplicate

    b. ECR

    c. triplicate

    d. NCR   *p256 6.2*

5 Which of the following pairs of 'fish dishes' would you expect to find on a 'full English breakfast' menu?

    a. flétan, anguille fumée

    b. bloaters, turbot

    c. kippers, merlan

    d. kedgeree, aiglefin fumé   *p246 6.1*

6 The type of checking system generally used at breakfast service is

    a. duplicate

    b. triplicate

    c. ECR

    d. a single order sheet   *p245 6.1*

7 The French term 'thé simple' means the guest has ordered

    a. tea only

    b. tea with a continental style breakfast

    c. tea with a full English breakfast

    d. tea with lemon   *p245 6.1*

8 The main difference between the service of 'full afternoon tea' and 'high tea' is that

    a. the menu for a 'full afternoon tea' is à la carte, whereas with 'high tea' it is table d'hôte

    b. with 'high tea' a cooked snack is offered

    c. with 'high tea' the tisanes would be offered

    d. 'high tea' is always served in the lounge
       area   *p253/254 6.2*

9 In the service of high tea what item always accompanies the service of the hot snack?

    a. cruet

    b. beverage

    c. buttered bread

    d. proprietary sauces   *p256 6.2*

10 Two of the most important factors to consider in the setting up for the service of a buffet tea are

a. prominent position – do you have sufficient equipment

b. ample space for guest circulation – the number of occasional tables required

c. ease of access to the wash-up – are there sufficient service staff

d. ease of access to the stillroom – prominent position   *p256/257 6.2*

11 The order of courses in a full afternoon tea menu is

a. hot toasted items – savoury sandwiches – buttered scones – gâteaux

b. buttered bread with preserves – pastries – toasted tea cakes – savoury sandwiches

c. assorted sandwiches – fruit bread and butter – gâteaux – hot buttered toast

d. pastries – brown and white buttered bread – assorted sandwiches – toasted crumpets   *p253 6.2*

12 Which of the following forks would be used in the lay-up of a cover for full afternoon tea?

a. sweet fork

b. pastry fork

c. fruit fork

d. joint fork   *p254 6.2*

13 At what stage in the service of full afternoon tea will the beverage be served?

a. before the gâteaux and pastries

b. before the buttered bread and preserves

c. before the toasted items

d. after the toasted items   *p256 6.2*

14   At breakfast the sugar usually offered with either tea or coffee
     would be

   a. granulated

   b. loaf

   c. castor

   d. demerara   *p249 6.1*

15   When the waiter is taking the breakfast order in the restaurant,
     how many sets of food/beverage checks will need to be written
     out?

   a. 1

   b. 4

   c. 3

   d. 2   *p251 6.1*

16   At what stage of the breakfast service in a restaurant would the
     beverage be placed on the table?

   a. at the commencement of the meal

   b. with the main course

   c. after the first course has been cleared

   d. after the main course has been served   *p251 6.1*

17   When the beverage is served at breakfast it will

   a. be placed to the right of the host

   b. be placed to the left of the host

   c. be placed at the head of the cover

   d. be silver served to all the guests   *p251 6.1*

18   After clearing the main course at breakfast the waiter should
     firstly

   a. crumb down

   b. take the order for the next course

   c. enquire if more toast, preserve, butter and beverage is required

   d. move the sideplate and sideknife in front of the guest   *p252 6.1*

19 Which of the following items would you *not* expect to find on a British breakfast menu?

   a. tisanes

   b. Café Hag

   c. Smoked eel

   d. croissants   *p246/247 6.1*

20 You would normally expect to find 'high tea' served in

   a. an outdoor catering operation

   b. a coffee shop

   c. a department store

   d. a first class hotel   *p254 6.2*

21 Which of the following would you *not* expect to find on a high tea menu?

   a. Welsh rarebit

   b. Buck rarebit

   c. Scotch Woodcock

   d. Châteaubriand   *p254 6.2*

22 The majority of items required in the service of a full English breakfast are set on the table during the mise-en-place period. List four items placed on the table after the guest has been seated   *p250 6.1*

23 Why does the cover laid for 'high tea' require a joint knife and fork?   *p254 6.2*

24 List two items that would only be set upon the table as part of the cover for full afternoon tea, once the guests had been seated   *p255 6.2*

25 List the items which make up the complete cover to be laid for the service of 'full afternoon tea'   *p254/255 6.2*

26 High tea offered in a departmental store means a choice from the normal afternoon tea menu plus a h . . s . . . . of some sort   *p254 6.2*

27 Two of the main advantages in the operation of a self-service breakfast buffet are the reduction in staff requirements and the flexibility it offers   *TRUE/FALSE*   *p252 6.1*

28 What is the purpose of a slop basin when setting a table in readiness for breakfast?   *p249/250 6.1*

29 What item of tableware from a full table d'hôte cover is *not* laid for breakfast?   *p249 6.1*

30 On a modern day 'English Breakfast Menu' we would expect to see such items as 'yoghurts, muesli, Flora margarine, and continental pastries'   *TRUE/FALSE*   *p246 6.1*

Answers . . . .

1 d,   2 b,   3 c,   4 a,   5 d,   6 a,   7 a,   8 b,   9 c,   10 d,
11a,   12 b,   13 c,   14 b,   15 d,   16 c,   17 a,   18 d,
19 c,   20 c,   21 d

22 Butter dish; preserve dish; jug of cold milk; toast rack/Roll Basket

23 Because a 'hot snack' is part of the high tea menu

24 Jug of cold milk; preserve dish

25 Sideplate; paper napkin; side or tea knife; pastry fork; teacup and saucer and teaspoon; slop basin and tea strainer; sugar basin and tongs; teapot and hot water jug stands or underplates; jug of cold milk; preserve dish with preserve spoon; ashtray

26 Hot snack

27 True

28 To hold the tea strainer and for 'slops' from teacups

29 Soup spoon

30 True

7. SPECIALISED FORMS OF SERVICE
(P 258–271)

1   At breakfast the 'main course' required by the floor waiter is prepared in the

    a. floor pantry

    b. kitchen

    c. stillroom

    d. larder   *p262 7.2*

2   In a five star hotel the floor service staff would be expected to deal with the service of

    a. continental and full English breakfasts

    b. breakfasts and afternoon tea's

    c. all requests for the provision of food and drink in rooms

    d. lunches and dinners   *p259 7.2*

3   All food and drink checks signed by a host to indicate services received should be immediately passed to

    a. the food and beverage manager

    b. the chef de cuisine

    c. the restaurant manager

    d. reception or control   *p260 7.2*

4   On taking the food order the floor waiter should retain the

    a. top copy

    b. duplicate copy

    c. flimsy or third copy

    d. both the flimsy and duplicate copies   *p260 7.2*

5   One of the main differences between laying a breakfast tray and a table for the service of breakfast is that

    a. underplates are usually omitted due to the lack of space

    b. lesser quality china is used in case of breakages

    c. breakfast trays cannot be laid up the night before

    d. disposables rather than linen would be used when laying up
       a breakfast tray   *p262 7.2*

6   Before transporting a 'breakfast tray' from the floor pantry to
      the guests room the last items placed upon the tray would be

    a. the toast and beverage

    b. any accompaniments required

    c. the butter and preserves

    d. the beverages ordered   *p262 7.2*

7   Mini bars are restocked

    a. after each guests visit

    b. each day

    c. weekly

    d. as required   *p264 7.2*

8   To ensure a resident is charged for a 'service' received in the
      lounge the chef de salle must

    a. ask the resident to sign the bill

    b. ask the resident for his room number

    c. ask the resident to pay cash

    d. ask the resident to sign the bill and indicate his room
       number   *p266 7.3*

9   The Ganymede Tray System originated in

    a. America

    b. Canada

    c. England

    d. France   *p267 7.4*

10   The Ganymede Tray System of food service relates to

a. industrial catering   c. school meals

b. hospital catering   d. store catering   *p267 7.4*

11   A 'commissary' is a term used in relation to

a. franchising

b. a member of the 'Portering' staff

c. airline catering

d. kosher catering   *p269 7.5*

12   For economy and tourist flights the style of food service carried out would be

a. trolley service

b. plate service

c. French style service

d. tray service   *p269 7.5*

13   'Cuisine 2000' is a term used in

a. fast food operations

b. rail catering services

c. welfare catering

d. flight catering   *p270 7.6*

14   In most instances the lounge service staff would collect any tea/coffee required for service in the lounge from

a. their own service pantry

b. the stillroom

c. the coffee shop

d. the buttery   *p265 7.3*

15 Distribution of weight is an important factor to consider when
    laying a breakfast tray   *TRUE/FALSE*   *p262 7.2*

16 Afternoon tea is the only meal served in the lounge
    TRUE/FALSE   *p265 7.3*

17 You are requested to lay a breakfast tray for the service of a
    continental breakfast with coffee (café complet). List all the
    equipment you would require   *p263 7.2*

18 The 'Dry Heat' system of food service used in hospitals is called
    the G. . . . . . . system   *p268 7.4*

19 When laying a breakfast tray one of the pieces of equipment
    required will be an ashtray   *TRUE/FALSE*   *p262 7.2*

20 List four of the main differences between laying up a breakfast
    tray and a table for the service of breakfasts   *p262 7.2*

21 List four factors to be considered when setting up a breakfast
    tray, to ensure efficiency and safety   *p262 7.2*

22 List six items that may come in a pre-portioned form when
    providing the requirements for a 'tea and coffee making' service
    in a guest's room   *p264 7.2*

23 As well as finding 'Lounge Service' in a five star hotel it may also
    be found in wine bars and on ships
    TRUE/FALSE   *p265 7.3*

24 Horlick's, Ovaltine, Bovril, coffee, cocoa, chocolate and tea are
    all hot beverages available to the guest should he require them in
    the lounge   *TRUE/FALSE*   *p266 7.3*

25 List four of the main advantages of the commercially available
    'tray service methods' used in hospital catering   *p268 7.4*

Answers . . . .

1 b,   2 c,   3 d,   4 c,   5 a,   6 a,   7 b,   8 d,   9 a,   10 b,
11 c,   12 d,   13 b,   14 b

15 True

16 False

17 Sideplate; sideknife; napkin; teacup, saucer and teaspoon;
sugar basin and tongs; coffee pot; hot milk pot; butterdish
with butter knife; preserve dish and spoon; toast rack/
underplate

18 Ganymede

19 False

20 Traycloth replaces the tablecloth; underplates omitted due to
lack of space; no table number; no ashtray

21 Even distribution of weight; spouts of the tea/coffee pots face
inwards; sauce bottles laid flat; correct positioning of items

22 Tea; coffee; creamer; chocolate; non-sugar sweetner;
biscuits; sugar

23 True

24 True

25 Meal presented appetisingly; labour and administration costs
cut; staff able to make better use of their time; patient able to
select meal from choice offered

8. GUÉRIDON SERVICE
(p272–320)

1   Guéridon service is said to have originated in

   a. France

   b. England

   c. Russia

   d. USA   *p273 8.1*

2   A guéridon is defined as a

   a. sideboard

   b. movable service table or trolley

   c. dumbwaiter

   d. carving trolley   *p273 8.1*

3   Which of the following pairs of fuel are best suited for use with a flare lamp?

   a. methylated spirits, petrol

   b. electricity, paraffin

   c. butane gas, methylated spirits

   d. paraffin, butane gas   *p274 8.1*

4   Which of the following selections of meat would always be carved very thinly?

   a. lamb and mutton

   b. pork and tongue

   c. veal and boiled beef

   d. beef and ham   *p282 8.3*

5   When filleting Dover sole at the guéridon the Dover sole should be filleted on a

   a. carving board   c. fish plate

   b. silver flat   d. joint plate *p290 8.4*

6   The first joint removed when carving chicken would be the

a. suprême

b. breast

c. leg

d. wing   *p302 8.4*

7   A guest orders a 'Châteaubriand'. A good food service operator will indicate to the guest that

a. the dish is only available when in season

b. there is a waiting time for this dish

c. this dish is always prepared 'saignant'

d. this dish is immediately available   *p294 8.4*

8   Which of the following types of 'steak' that might be ordered by a guest would not require you to ask 'How would you wish your steak cooked?'

a. steak tartare

b. porterhouse steak

c. entrecôte steak

d. filet steak   *p295 8.4*

9   What spirit of liqueur would you use to flambée steak Diane?

a. cognac

b. rum

c. vodka

d. kirsch   *p296 8.4*

10   The proportions of oil to vinegar when preparing French dressing are

a. 2 to 1   c. 4 to 1

b. 3 to 1   d. equal quantities   *p299 8.4*

11 One of the main ingredients in an acidulated cream dressing is
    a. olive oil
    b. sour cream
    c. fresh lemon juice
    d. malt vinegar   *p300 8.4*

12 Salade niçoise contains
    a. diced apple and celery
    b. hearts of lettuce and hard boiled egg
    c. orange segments, skinned grapes, sliced banana
    d. tomato, French beans, olives, and sliced potato
                                                         p302 8.4

13 Which of the following joints is recognised from its menu
    description as a boned sirloin of beef?
    a. carbonnade de boeuf
    b. kari de boeuf
    c. aloyau de boeuf
    d. contrefilet de boeuf   *p308 8.4*

14 Which of the following sets of flambée dishes require brandy as
    the flaming agent?
    a. pineapple flambée, cerises flambée
    b. banane flambée, crêpe Suzette
    c. crêpe Suzette, pêche flambée
    d. cerises flambée, banane flambée   *p313/318 8.4*

15 Which of the accompaniments offered with the menu dish
    'tortue vrai aux Xeres' would be added at the guéridon?
    a. fresh cream   c. beetroot juice
    b. sherry   d. grated parmesan cheese   *p289 8.4*

16 From which of the following game would it be correct to carve the breast?

a. grouse

b. bécasse

c. faisan

d. bécassine   *p308 8.4*

17 It is correct when preparing fresh pineapple on the guéridon to

a. remove the outer rind and then the centre core

b. remove the outer rind only

c. remove the centre core first and then the rind

d. skin the whole pineapple and then slice as
    required   *p318 8.4*

18 The type of menu presented to the guest where guéridon service takes place is usually

a. carte du jour

b. table d'hôte

c. à la carte

d. French classical menu   *p273 8.1*

19 Which of the following menu terms is the odd one out?

a. entrecôte

b. porterhouse

c. Châteaubriand

d. darne   *p292/293 8.4*

20 What is the French menu term denoting a 'leg/thigh' of pork?

a. épaule

b. selle

c. cuissot

d. gigot   *p312 8.4*

21 The term 'carré d'agneau rôti' on an à la carte menu denotes

    a. roast shoulder of lamb

    b. roast leg of lamb

    c. roast saddle of lamb

    d. roast best end of lamb   *p309 8.4*

22 Grouse would always be served whole   *TRUE/FALSE*
                                                 p307 8.4

23 The Suzette pan used in guéridon service is usually made of silver plated copper. What is the reason for this?   *p275 8.1*

24 List four items of equipment used in conjunction with guéridon service that may be regarded as 'selling aids'   *p277 8.2*

25 If the guests seated at your table are a family of father, mother, son and daughter, in what order should they be served?
                                                 p277 8.2

26 When taking the order at the table r.......... of the h... is an important factor in effective communication   *p277 8.2*

27 The guéridon should be kept in one position for the service of a complete course and not moved from guest to guest
TRUE/FALSE   *p279 8.2*

Answers ....

1 a, 2 b, 3 c, 4 d, 5 d, 6 c, 7 b, 8 a, 9 a, 10 b,
11 c, 12 d, 13 d, 14 c, 15 d, 16 c, 17 a, 18 c,
19 d, 20 c, 21 d

22 False

23 This gives an even distribution of heat

24 Carving trolley; hors-d'oeuvre trolley; sweet trolley; liqueur trolley

25 Mother; daughter; son; father (host)

26 Recognition of the host

27 True

9. FUNCTION CATERING
(p321–350)

1   'Banqueting' is a term used to cover the service of special functions which might be held in

    a. the lounge

    b. the coffee shop

    c. rooms set aside for the purpose

    d. a hotel's various restaurants   *p392 9.1*

2   Which of the following groups of functions would you expect to take place in the banqueting rooms of an establishment?

    a. cocktail party, charity dinner, hunt ball

    b. wedding breakfast, full afternoon tea, dinner dance

    c. floor service, seminars, conferences

    d. full English breakfasts, buffet tea's, special promotions   *p322 9.1*

3   The prime function of the 'sales administration manager' is to

    a. organise the efficient running of all special functions

    b. sell an establishments facilities and services

    c. compile and cost the menu's required for various events

    d. employ and control casual staff for special functions   *p323 9.1*

4   Which of the following list of points is it most essential for the banqueting manger to have available/know when opening initial discussions with a client concerning the booking of a function?

    a. availability of a toastmaster, licensing requirements, cash or credit facilities, time of arrival

    b. sets of table plans, room capacities, banqueting booking diary, sound relay systems

    c. cocktail list, banqueting wine list, various banqueting menu's, availability of floral decor

    d. banqueting booking diary, banqueting wine list, sample banquet menu's, availability of accommodation
           p324 9.1/p329 9.2

5   Communication between the banqueting administration staff
    and other departments servicing a function is by means of a

    a. regular senior staff meeting

    b. function list

    c. banqueting memorandum

    d. banqueting instruction sheet   *p324 9.1/p332 9.2*

6   **A** A silver service food   **B** A banqueting wine waiter
         waiter at a banquet is   will generally be expected to
         generally expected to   serve at least
         serve
                                                      a. 20 covers
         a. 10 covers
                                                      b. 25 covers
         b. 14 covers
                                                      c. 30 covers
         c. 18 covers
                                                      d. 35 covers
         d.   6 covers   *p326/327 9.1*

7   At a formal function the table running off at right angles from
    the top table is termed a

    a. station

    b. branch

    c. arm

    d. sprig   *p335/338 9.3*

8   At a formal dinner the person always served first on the top
    table would be

    a. the guest of honour

    b. the host

    c. the guest of honour's wife

    d. the function organiser   *p343 9.3*

9   In banquet service, once the stations have been allocated, the food service staff will all be numbered so that

   a. the banqueting manager can check and confirm that he has sufficient staff to man all the 'stations'

   b. the wages clerk can allocate 'wages' quickly at the conclusion of the function

   c. the waiter with a station furthest from the service entrance will be nearer the head of the queue at the hotplate

   d. the service of both food and wine is carried out in a more orderly fashion in the room   *p339 9.3*

10   Which of the following would be the most appropriate order of courses for a special function?

   a. hors d'oeuvre – fish – meat – sweet – coffee

   b. egg – meat – fish – sweet – coffee

   c. fish – meat – savoury – sweet – coffee

   d. farinaceous – meat – savoury – cheese – coffee   *p333 9.2*

11   The minimum distance between two 'sprigs', for safety reasons, should be

   a. 2 metres

   b. 1 metre

   c. 3 metres

   d. 1½ metres   *p334 9.2*

12   When the banqueting food service staff queue at the hotplate, who should be at the head of the queue?

   a. the waiter whose station is furthest away

   b. the eldest member of the food service staff

   c. the top table waiter

   d. the banqueting head water in order to control the service   *p339 9.3*

13 At a wedding breakfast the 'toasts' and other formalities will
    normally take place under the direction of

    a. the bridegroom and the best man

    b. the toastmaster and the bridegroom

    c. the best man and the toastmaster

    d. the bride's father and the bridegroom   *p347 9.4*

14 The host's at a wedding function are usually

    a. best man and matron of honour

    b. bride and bridegroom

    c. bridegroom's parents

    d. bride's parents   *p347/348 9.4*

15 Traditionally the first toast proposed at a wedding function is
    always to the

    a. bride and bridegroom

    b. the bridesmaids

    c. the matron of honour

    d. the bride's parents   *p348 9.4*

16 The room allowance per person for a sit down style function is
    said to be in the region of

    a. 2–3 sq. metres

    b. 1–1.4 sq. metres

    c. 0.5–1 sq. metre

    d. 0.75–1 sq. metres   *p334 9.2/p344 9.4*

17 In the setting up of a reception tea the ends of the buffet should
    be

    a. put flush with the wall to minimise the use of linen

    b. left open for ease of access

    c. box pleated with the buffet cloth

    d. hidden by the use of floral decor   *p344 9.4*

18 When clothing up the buffet the cloth should fall to within

   a. two inches of the ground

   b. half an inch of the ground

   c. an inch of the ground

   d. just touch the ground   *p344 9.4*

19 Petit fours would be offered with

   a. hors-d'oeuvre

   b. the sorbet

   c. coffee

   d. an aperitif   *p333 9.2*

20 The minimum size of a banqueting/buffet cloth is recognised to be

   a. 2 metres × 2 metres

   b. 2 metres × 4 metres

   c. 2 metres × 6 metres

   d. 2 metres × 8 metres   *p335 9.2*

21 The average width of a cover around the circumference of a round table is two feet   *TRUE/FALSE*   *p337 9.3*

22 The wine waiters at a special function often work by a 'float system'. What do you understand by this?   *p327 9.1*

23 In banqueting it is usually accepted that on specimen luncheon and dinner menu's offered to a potential host there will only be a limited choice   *TRUE/FALSE*   *p333 9.2*

24 Indicate the order in which the 'receiving' line should be made up at a wedding function   *p348 9.4*

25 Who replies to the toast proposed to the bridesmaids?   *p348 9.4*

26 List four factors that need to be discussed with the host, that would appear on the banqueting memorandum and relate specifically to a wedding function   *p344 9.4*

27 After the initial reception, all adults, regardless of official titles or rank, should be addressed as 's . .' or 'm. . . .' with the exception of female members of the Royal Family who should be addressed as 'm . . .'   *p341 9.3*

28 Give the definition of the term 'friandises'   *p333 9.2*

29 Why would the banqueting manager request that at least three/four copies of a table plan should be made available for a formal dinner function?   *p335 9.3*

30 At the regular Friday meeting on future business you, as Restaurant Manger, are informed that there is to be a special party for dinner on the following Friday and the restaurant will be closed to other customers

   a. List *three* of the most important pieces of information required to successfully plan for the function   *p329 9.2*

   b. List *three* of the most important supervisory actions to be taken on the day of the function, prior to the commencement of service   *p339 9.3*

Answers . . . .

1 c,   2 a,   3 b,   4 d,   5 c,   6 A a,   B b,   7 d,   8 b,   9 c,
10 a,   11 a,   12 c,   13 c,   14 d,   15 a,   16 b,   17 c,
18 b,   19 c,   20 b

21 True

22 The wine waiter starts service with a 'float' – pays for drinks on
receipt from the dispense bar from his float – collects cash from
guests upon delivery of an order – and is able to give change – at
end of service hands in float

23 False

24 Bride's father; brides mother; bride; bridegroom;
bridegroom's father; bridegroom's mother; best man;
matron of honour

25 The 'best man'

26 Wedding cake; display of presents; room required for
changing; services of a photographer

27 'Sir' or 'madam'; 'maam'

28 Sweet meats – often termed Petit Fours – and offered with coffee

29 1 to organise for checking purposes prior to function; 2/3
available to guests in reception area to check where they are
seated; 4 to banqueting manager for reference/file

30 a. Number of covers; time of arrival/dinner; nature of the
occasion

    b. Staff instruction sheet to brief staff on procedures; allotting
staff to top table and other stations; order of line-up at the
hotplate – top table first

10. SUPERVISORY ASPECTS OF FOOD AND BEVERAGE SERVICE
(p351–392)

1 The modern trend in control systems is to use

a. CFA

b. ECR

c. HCIMA

d. HCTC   *p369 10.2*

2 If an hotel resident is served 'full afternoon tea' in the lounge, they will normally

a. pay by credit card

b. pay cash

c. ask for the cost to be added to the hotel bill

d. sign the bill for the service received   *p366 10.2*

3 Who receives the top copy of a 'drink check'?

a. cashier

b. control department

c. kept by the sommelier

d. issuing department   *p213 5.6/p364 10.2*

4 When alcoholic beverages are delivered to an establishment they will usually be accompanied by a

a. delivery note

b. requisition sheet

c. credit note

d. statement   *p374 10.3*

5   The main difference between an invoice and a delivery note is that

   a. the prices charged are only shown on the invoice

   b. the invoice is usually received by the purchaser prior to delivery

   c. the delivery note is usually printed in red

   d. discounts agreed are indicated on the delivery note   *p375 10.3*

6   All alcoholic beverage stock delivered should be checked by the receiver against the

   a. copy order and requisition form

   b. copy order only

   c. delivery note only

   d. delivery note and copy order   *p375 10.3*

7   The requisition form should be signed by

   a. the cellarman

   b. the sommelier

   c. someone in authority

   d. the chef d'étage   *p373 10.3*

8   The main purpose of a 'bin card' is to show, for control reasons, the

   a. balance in stock and the total cash value of a particular item

   b. balance remaining in stock, at any given time, of a particular item

   c. total amount of issues of a certain item

   d. total amount of receipts of a certain item   *p376 10.3*

9   The term used to indicate beer wasted when cleaning pipes, or from broken bottles, or spillage, is

   a. ullage   c. wort

   b. mash   d. grist   *p371 10.3*

10 A '6 out' spirit measure denotes

    a. ½ of a gill

    b. ¼ of a gill

    c. ⅓ of a gill

    d. ⅙ of a gill   *p358 10.1*

11 Which of the following groups of drinks are usually served using a '3 out' measure?

    a. port, sherry, vermouth, liqueurs

    b. vermouth, gin, vodka, liqueurs

    c. sherry, port, Noilly Prat, Cinzano

    d. brandy, rum, sweet Martini, Madeira   *p358 10.1*

12 The maximum number of 'licensing sessions' held, apart from the annual licensing meeting that is held in February, would be

    a. 4

    b. 6

    c. 8

    d. 10   *p352 10.1*

13 The capacity of an average size bottle of wine is

    a. 55cl

    b. 65cl

    c. 75cl

    d. 85cl   *p359 10.1*

14 Stocktaking should take place

    a. if time allows

    b. at the conclusion of each days business

    c. on a monthly basis

    d. if 'fiddling' is suspected   *p371 10.3*

15 The 'annual licensing meeting' is always held in the month of

   a. February

   b. April

   c. December

   d. October   *p352 10.1*

16 The type of 'justices' licence that allows a licensee to sell all
   types of alcoholic liquor for consumption 'on' and 'off' the
   premises is known as

   a. a restricted 'on' licence

   b. a 'full' on licence

   c. a combined licence

   d. a Part IV licence   *p352 10.1*

17 The type of licence granted by the liquor licensing magistrates
   allowing a person to purchase an alcoholic beverage for
   consumption with a table meal is a

   a. justices licence

   b. residential licence

   c. restaurant licence

   d. occasional licence   *p353 10.1*

18 A combined licence is granted for premises which fulfil the
   conditions required for both a

   a. part IV licence and a Justices licence

   b. residential licence and an 'on' licence

   c. restaurant licence and a Supper Hour Certificate

   d. residential licence and a restaurant licence   *p353 10.1*

19 The time allowed in a licensed restaurant at the end of the
   normal permitted hours for the consumption of alcoholic liquor
   with a meal is

   a. 30 minutes   c. 45 minutes

   b. 1 hour   d. 10 minutes   *p355 10.1*

20 A resident in licensed premises is allowed to purchase and
consume alcoholic liquor

   a. only within the permitted hours

   b. at any time

   c. only with a table meal

   d. as long as cash is paid with the order   *p355 10.1*

21 The period of time allowed at the end of the morning and
evening periods of the permitted hours, as 'drinking up' time, is

   a. 20 minutes

   b. 15 minutes

   c. 10 minutes

   d. 30 minutes   *p355 10.1*

22 A young person, over 16 years of age and under 18 years of age,
if consuming a substantial meal in licensed premises, would be
allowed to purchase and consume

   a. any form of alcoholic beverage

   b. beer, cider and perry only

   c. beer and cider only

   d. no alcoholic beverages   *p359 10.1*

23 The permitted hours for 'off-licensed premises' commence at

   a. 08.00 am

   b. 08.30 am

   c. 09.00 am

   d. 10.00 am   *p355 10.1*

24 A club in which intoxicating liquor is supplied must apply to a
magistrates court for a certificate of registration to be renewed

   a. every 3 months   c. every 9 months

   b. every 6 months   d. annually   *p352 10.1*

25 The 'permitted hours' on a weekday, in licensed premises, are a total of

   a. 8 hours

   b. 9 hours

   c. 10 hours

   d. 12 hours   *p355 10.1*

26 A 'returns book' is a document used to record

   a. the amounts of VAT payable to the tax office

   b. the number of empty kegs, casks, bottles and crates sent back to the brewery

   c. the daily takings from the bars

   d. a return list of regular customers   *p371 10.3*

27 The type of licence/certificate granted to a licence holder for social functions held on unlicensed premises would be

   a. a justices' licence

   b. an extended hours certificate

   c. an occasional licence

   d. a special hours certificate   *p354 10.1*

28 The variation to the basic permitted hours which allows a licence to be exempted from the normal permitted hours during a certain day, or for a certain time, is the

   a. special hours certificate

   b. general order of exemption

   c. special order of exemption

   d. extended hours certificate   *p355/356 10.1*

29 An establishment holding a supper hour certificate is allowed to sell alcoholic beverages for consumption with a table meal, beyond the normal permitted hours, for a period of

   a. 90 minutes

   b. 30 minutes

   c. one hour

   d. two hours   *p356 10.1*

30 Licensed premises may be classified according to the way in which they are controlled. This may be by three methods

   a. publican – manager – tenant

   b. managed – tenanted – free house

   c. owner of a free house – manager – the controlling brewery

   d. tenant – the controlling brewery – franchised

                                                                   p358 10.1

31 At the conclusion of service the cashier transfers the information from the duplicate bills on to a

   a. statement

   b. balance sheet

   c. petty cash sheet

   d. summary sheet   *p365 10.2*

32 What are the three new types of licence (Part IV Licenses) created by the 1961 Licensing Act, and coming under the title of 'Restricted on-licenses'   *p353 10.1*

33 Indicate the Sunday opening hours (permitted hours) for England and Wales   *p355 10.1*

34 It is an offence for a young person under 18 to consume alcoholic liquor in a bar   *TRUE/FALSE*   *p359 10.1*

35 What licence would you be holding where there are no 'licensing hour' restrictions?   *p353 10.1*

36 What is the definition of the term 'brewsters' sessions?   *p352 10.1*

37 Indicate the purpose of 'maximum' and 'minimum' stock as shown on a bin card   *p373 10.3/p376 10.3*

38 What is the purpose of a requisitions form?   *p373 10.3*

39 All draught beer should be served in a government stamped glass of either 25 or 50 centilitres capacity   *TRUE/FALSE*
                                                                            p224 5.8

40 It is an offence for under 18s to attempt to purchase alcoholic liquor on licensed premises   *TRUE/FALSE*   *p359 10.1*

41 Indicate three variations to the normal permitted hours which allow for half-hour 'drinking-up' time   *p357 10.1*

42 The legal use of a '6 out' measure or optic applies to the service of certain spirits only. What are these spirits?   *p358 10.1*

43 How many glasses of whisky may be served from one pint of whisky, when a '6 out' spirit measure is used?   *p358 10.1*

44 The approximate capacity of an average size bottle of wine is 75 centilitres   *TRUE/FALSE*   *p359 10.1*

45 The number of 125 ml glasses of wine obtainable from one average size bottle of wine is eight   *TRUE/FALSE*
                                                                            p359 10.1

46 List four of the main reasons why a control system is necessary in a food service area   *p364 10.2*

47 If a resident ordered drink in the lounge area and did not wish to pay cash what procedure should take place?   *p366 10.2*

48 The object of a daily duty rota is to ensure that all the necessary duties are covered in order that efficient service may be carried out   *TRUE/FALSE*   *p386 10.6*

49 Where a waiter billing machine is in operation, for control purposes each waiter has their own control key
    TRUE/FALSE   *p369 10.2*

50 In what circumstances would it be necessary to obtain an 'occasional licence' for a special function?   *p354 10.1*

51 What is the definition of the word 'ullage'?   *p371 10.3*

52 What is the meaning of the term 'par' stock?   *p374 10.3*

53 A 'contract' is made when one party agrees to the terms of an offer made by another party   *TRUE/FALSE*   *p359 10.1*

54 The 'Sale of Goods Act' came into force in 1989 and applies to the sale of goods by description   *TRUE/FALSE*
          p360 10.1

55 List four 'Acts/Regulations' which affect health and safety issues to both staff and visitors on your premises?   *p362 10.1*

56 A cheque card is used primarily to save writing a cheque and allows you to obtain money when banks are closed
TRUE/FALSE   *p367 10.2*

57 What are the three recognised 'elements of cost'?
          p378 10.4

58 What is the object of providing a 'duty rota' for your staff?   *p386 10.6*

59 How would you define the term a 'training need'?   *p387 10.6*

60 Your 'job description' may be described as a broad statement of the purpose, scope, duties and responsibilities of a particular job   *TRUE/FALSE*   *p389 10.6*

61 The following information is based on a 120 seater restaurant

    Operational hours
    The restaurant is open six days a week all year

    Opening hours
    12 noon to 2pm   Lunch Service
    7pm to 10pm   Dinner Service

    Average customer numbers
    Lunch – 40
    Dinner – 75

Average customer spending

	Food	Drink
Lunch	£6 per head	£3 per head
Dinner	£10 per head	£5 per head

Staffing establishment
Lunch – one member of staff per 10 customers
Dinner – one member of staff per 15 customers
All staff are employed for the entire service period plus one hour prior to the service and one hour after the service
Staff wages are paid at £3 per hour

Costs
The total overhead cost for one year is estimated at 20% of the total annual revenue (food and drink)
The food costs are 40% of the annual food revenue
The drink costs are 50% of the annual drink revenue

Using the above information calculate the following:
a. i.   The annual revenue for food
    ii. The annual revenue for drink
    iii. The annual revenue for lunch
    iv. The annual revenue for dinner
    v.   The total annual revenue

b. The total number of staff needed each day for the service of
    i.   lunch
    ii   dinner

c. The total annual wage costs

d. The percentage of wage costs in relation to the total annual revenue

e. The average daily percentage seat occupancy during the year for
    i.   lunch
    ii. dinner

f. The average daily overhead costs for each day of operation

g. Calculate the gross profit cash and percentage for the year for
    i.   food
    ii. drink
    iii. total (food and drink)

h. The total amount of money left over at the end of the year after all costs have been deducted and its percentage of the total revenue (net profit)　　　　　　　　*p377–380 10.4*

Answers . . . .

1 b,　2 d,　3 d,　4 a,　5 a,　6 d,　7 c,　8 b,　9 a,　10 d,
11 c,　12 c,　13 c,　14 c,　15 a,　16 b,　17 c,　18 d,
19 a,　20 b,　21 a,　22 b,　23 a,　24 d,　25 d,　26 b,
27 c,　28 b,　29 c,　30 b,　31 d

32　Restaurant licence; residential licence; combined licence

33　12.00–3.00pm, 7.00–10.30pm (Total of 6½ hours)

34　True

35　Residential licence

36　The name given to the Annual Licensing meeting held in the first fortnight in February

37　Maximum stock tells you how much to reorder; minimum stock determines your reordering level

38　To control the movement of items from the cellar and into the dispensing units and to avoid overstocking the bar

39　True

40　True

41　General Order of Exemption; Special Order of Exemption; Supper Hour Certificate; Special Hours Certificate; Extended Hours Certificate

42　Whisky; Gin; Vodka; Rum

43　24 glasses

44　True

45　False

46 Controls items issued from various departments; should reduce to a minimum pilfering and wastage; to ensure the client's bill is made out correctly; to give a breakdown of sales and income received

47 Resident should be requested to sign for the services received

48 True

49 True

50 To sell 'alcoholic liquor' on unlicensed premises

51 Beer returned to brewery – ie spillage/broken bottles/waste in pipes

52 The level of stock held in a bar is known as 'par' stock

53 True

54 False

55 Occupiers Liability Act 1957; Health & Safety at Work Act 1974; Fire Precaution Act 1971; Food Hygiene Regulations

56 False

57 Labour; food and beverage costs; overheads

58 To ensure all the necessary duties are covered and to provide the basis for staff training

59 The 'gap' between the work standards of an employee and those standards required by the employer

60 True

61 a. i.   The annual revenue for food

Lunch food revenue
= spend per head × number of covers × number of days × number of weeks
= £6 × 40 covers × 6 days × 52 weeks
= £74880

Dinner food revenue
= spend per head × number of covers × number of days × number of weeks
= £10 × 75 covers × 6 days × 52 weeks
= £234000

Total annual food revenue
= lunch food revenue + dinner food revenue
= £74880 + £234000
= £308880

a. ii. The annual revenue for drink

Lunch drink revenue
= spend per head × number of covers × number of days × number of weeks
= £3 × 40 covers × 6 days × 52 weeks
= £37440

Dinner drink revenue
= spend per head × number of covers × number of days × number of weeks
= £5 × 75 covers × 6 days × 52 weeks
= £117000

Total annual drink revenue
= lunch drink revenue + dinner drink revenue
= £37440 + £117000
= £154440

a. iii. Total annual revenue for lunch
= annual lunch drink revenue + annual lunch food revenue
= £37440 + £74880
= £112320

a. iv. Total annual revenue for dinner
= annual dinner drink revenue + annual dinner food revenue
= £117000 + £234000
= £351000

a. v. Total annual revenue
= annual lunch revenue + annual dinner revenue
= £112320 + £351000
= £463320

OR

= annual drink revenue + annual food revenue
= £154440 + £308880
= £463320

b. The total number of staff needed for each day for the service of:

i. Lunch
    one member of staff is required for ten customers
    the average number of customers per day 40

    therefore the average number of staff for lunch $= \dfrac{40}{10} = 4$

ii. Dinner
    one member of staff is required for 15 customers
    the average number of customers per day $= 75$

    therefore the average number of staff for dinner $= \dfrac{75}{15} = 5$

c. Total annual wage costs

Lunch wage costs per day
= number of staff × working hours × rate per hour
= 4 staff × 4 hours × £3
= £48

Dinner wage costs per day
= number of staff × working hours × rate per hour
= 5 staff × 5 hours × £3
= £75

Total wage costs per day
= lunch wage costs + dinner wage costs
= £48 + £75
= £123

Total annual wage costs
= total wage costs per day × number of days × number of weeks
= £123 × 6 × 52
= £38376

d. Percentage of wage cost in relation to total revenue

$$\text{Wage cost percentage} = \frac{\text{Wage costs}}{\text{Revenue}} \times 100$$

$$= \frac{£38376}{£463320} \times 100$$

$$= 8.28\%$$

e. The average daily percentage seat occupancy during the year
    for:
    i.   Lunch

    Lunch percentage seat occupancy $= = \dfrac{\text{covers actual}}{\text{covers available}} \times 100$

    $= \dfrac{40}{120} \times 100$

    $= 33.34\%$

    ii. Dinner

    Dinner percentage seat occupancy $= \dfrac{\text{covers actual}}{\text{covers available}} \times 100$

    $= \dfrac{75}{120} \times 100$

    $= 62.50\%$

f. The average daily overhead cost
    Overheads = 20% of revenue

    therefore total annual overheads $= \dfrac{20}{100} \times £463320$

    $= £92660$

    Daily overheads costs $= \dfrac{\text{annual cost}}{6 \text{ days} \times 52 \text{ weeks}}$

    $= \dfrac{£92664}{312}$

    $= £297$ per day

g. The gross profit cash and percentage for the year for:
    i.   Food cash gross profit and percentage
         Food cost = 40% of total food revenue
         therefore gross profit = 60% of total food revenue

         gross profit on food $= \dfrac{60}{100} \times £308880$

         $= £185328$ cash, 60%

ii. Drink cash gross profit and percentage
Drink cost = 50% of total drink revenue
therefore gross profit = 50% of total drink revenue

$$\text{gross profit on drink} = \frac{50}{100} \times £154440$$

= £77220 cash, 50%

iii. Total cash gross profit and percentage
Total cash gross profit = food gross profit + drink gross profit
= £185328 + £77220
= £262548

$$\text{Percentage gross profit} = \frac{\text{cash gross profit}}{\text{revenue}} \times 100$$

$$= \frac{£262548}{£463320} \times 100$$

= 56.67%

h. The total amount of money left over at the end of the year after all costs have been deducted and its percentage of total revenue (net profit)
Net profit = gross profit − (labour costs + overhead costs)
= £262548 − (£38376 + £92664)
= £131508
Net profit as a percentage of revenue

$$= \frac{\text{net profit}}{\text{revenue}} \times 100$$

$$= \frac{£131508}{£463320} \times 100$$

= 28.38%

Check matrix	£	%		£	%
Costs	200772	43.34	Costs	200772	43.34
Labour	38376	8.28			
Overheads	92664	20.00	Gross profit	262548	56.66
Net profit	131508	28.38			
Revenue	463320	100.00	Revenue	463320	100.00

11. COMPETENCE IN FOOD AND BEVERAGE SERVICE

There are a wide variety of skills, tasks and duties in food and beverage service. The extent of skills required will depend on the type of operation and the level of service provided. The competence statements below are general lists from which specific requirements may be selected and further detailed according to the establishments requirements. *p20–21*

Interpersonal skills
The practitioner should be able to:
– maintain a professional attitude to colleagues and
  guests   *p17–19 1.8*
– contribute to the development of team work within the food and
  beverage department
– address guests appropriately
– have sufficient knowledge of the menu, service requirements,
  services offered to be able to deal with guest enquiries
– operate under the establishment routines for dealing with
  complaints, accidents, special requests and policies on provision of
  services   *p177–184 5.2*

Taking bookings
The practitioner should be able to:
– demonstrate ability in taking bookings, by letter, in person and
  over the phone
– Have knowledge of the services provided by the establishment,
  opening times, menus, prices
– operate within the constraints of the establishment, for instance,
  requiring confirmation, not overbooking and taking special
  request information   *p184/185 5.3*

Preparation for service
The practitioner should be able to:
– carry out a variety of preparatory tasks and duties within the food
  and beverage service areas. These include:
      housekeeping duties,
      setting out of tables and chairs and other equipment,
      handling linen and paper items,
      clothing up,
      laying up,
      preparing the stillroom,

cleaning and polishing of crockery, cutlery and glassware,
stocking of sideboards and other storage areas including
hotplates,
the setting up of buffets,
preparation of a variety of trolleys for service,
preparation for a variety of service methods,
preparation of bar areas   *p185/202 5.4*

Receiving of guests
The practitioner should be able to:
– meet greet and seat guests within the service area
– take note of and action upon guest requirements
– direct and advise guests within a variety of service situations
                                                           p184–185 5.3

Taking orders for food and drink
The practitioner should be able to:
– state the requirement for the efficient taking of orders in a variety
  of differing service situations
– demonstrate ability in the taking of orders from guests according
  to the establishments procedures
– have knowledge of, and be able to provide explanations of the
  items on offer and the service requirements
– have the ability to identify individual guest's orders after the whole
  order has been taken   *p203–205 5.6*

The service of food
The practitioner should be able to:
– demonstrate practical ability in basic technical skills including the
  stacking and carrying of trays, the use of salvers and service plates,
  the use of a spoon and fork and other service equipment, the
  carrying of glassware
– demonstrate appropriate skills for a variety of service situations
– observe normal service conventions within the service area
– serve a variety of foods using appropriate skills and hygienic and
  safe working practices
– demonstrate a logical and efficient working method
– deal with guest requirements and special requests as they arise
– contribute to the team working requirements of the establishment
– adopt appropriate liaison with other staff working within the food
  and beverage department   *p213–219 5.7*

The service of alcoholic bar beverages and cigars

The practitioner should be able to:

— demonstrate practical ability in basic technical skills including carrying glasses, opening of wine bottles and other drink containers, pouring skills, the use of trays, the carrying of glassware
— demonstrate appropriate skills for a variety of service situations
— observe normal service conventions within the service area
— observe the legal requirements for the service of alcoholic beverages
— serve a variety of alcoholic drinks using appropriate skills and hygienic and safe working practices
— serve cigarettes and cigars according to the guests requirements
— demonstrate a logical and efficient working method
— deal with guest requirements and special requests as they arise
— contribute to the team working requirements of the establishment
— adopt appropriate liaison with other staff working within the food and beverage department   *p219–227 5.8*

The service of non-alcoholic beverages

The practitioner should be able to:

— demonstrate practical ability in basic technical skills
— demonstrate appropriate skills for a variety of service situations
— observe normal service conventions within the service area
— prepare and serve a variety of non-alcoholic drinks using appropriate skills and hygienic and safe working practices
— demonstrate a logical and efficient working method
— deal with guest requirements and special requests as they arise
— contribute to the team working requirements of the establishment
— adopt appropriate liaison with other staff working within the food and beverage department   *p227–231 5.9*

Clearing

The practitioner should be able to:

— demonstrate appropriate skills in the clearing of guest's tables and food and beverage service areas
— demonstrate the skills of clearing by hand and onto trays having regard for the guests convenience and adopting hygienic and safe working practices
— demonstrate a logical and efficient working method
— contribute to the team working requirements of the establishment
— adopt appropriate liaison with other staff working within the food and beverage department   *p231–238 5.10*

Billing and cashiering

The practitioner should be able to:
- carry out billing procedures for a variety of service situations
- observe the establishment's requirements for security and credit allowances
- undertake cashiering duties according to the establishment requirements
- handle a variety of payment methods
- complete point of sale control requirements including the preparation of summary sheets and other reports

p238–242 5.11/p364–371 10.2

Clearing following service

The practitioner should be able to:
- demonstrate appropriate skills required in the clearing of a variety of service areas
- adopt safe and hygienic working practices
- ensure the security requirements of the establishment are maintained
- adopt the appropriate action for the storage of food items
- contribute to the development of a good working team

p242–243 5.12

CROSSWORDS

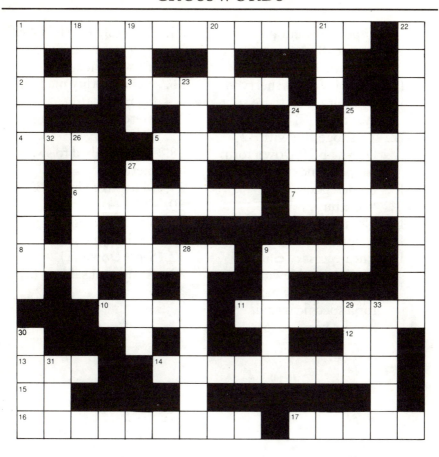

Across

1. Double fillet steak (13)
2. A smoked one may be served as an hors-d'oeuvre (3)
3. A sweet dish . . . Creole (6)
4. A 'BAD' one of these may cause complaints (3) (Anagram)
5. Qualification of a good waiter (10)
6. A cutlet – but not of meat (7)
7. A commodity made from sugar cane (5)

Down

1. Floor waiter (10)
9. See 12 Across (5)
18. Used as a flavouring agent (3)
19. A Dutch cheese (4)
20. Card used in cellar control (3)
21. 4½ gallons backwards (3)
22. Preparation beforehand (4-2-5)
23. Used in buffet work (5)
24. 30 Down plus this may be served as an hors-d'oeuvre (4-4)

8. Type of restaurant service (8)
9. Serviette fold (4)
10. Term for a dry sherry (4)
11. Restaurant staff are split into these (7)
12. This together with 32 Down and 9 Down form a type of menu (1, 2, 5)
13. French goose (3)
14. Wine butler (9)
15. Not the 'out' door (2)
16. A boned sirloin steak (9)
17. The necessary china, glass and tableware needed for one person for a specific meal is known as a . . . (5)

25. A complete dish in itself – served as received from kitchen (6)
26. A commodity made from milk (6)
27. Method of cleaning silver (7)
28. Term applied to sweet sherry (7)
29. Made from hops (3)
30. Offal (4)
31. Type of catering establishment (3)
32. See 9 Down (1)
33. A cutlet of salmon (5)

Across

1. Accompaniment served with a class of soup (8)
6. Chump . . . ? (4)
8. Tropical fruit from the West Indies (5)
10. Part of an oyster cruet (7)
11. Served in a demi-tasse (4)
12. Made from fuggles and goldings (4)
13. . . . sauté turbigo (6)
14. Second copy (9)
15. An abbreviation of Overproof (2)

Down

1. French cheese from Normandy (9)
2. System of collecting waiter's gratuities (5)
3. 4½ gallons backwards (3)
4. All spirits are this (2)
5. French term for a 'clearing' waiter (12)
6. A long leaf lettuce (3)
7. Type of sweet sherry (7)
9. Root vegetable in French (5)

16. Fish used in the making of hors-d'oeuvres (4)
17. Hunting sauce (8)
20. French goose (3)
21. Used in risotto (4)
23. Natural mineral water (7)
25. Spanish town famous for sherry (5)
26. This soup is served with the following accompaniments – cheese straws, brown bread and butter, half lemon, warm sherry (6)

10. Mexican spirit obtained from cactus plant (7)
14. A cut from a round fish (5)
16A. Cross between a grapefruit and tangerine (4)
17. 'Fillers' and 'binders' are parts of one of these (5)
18. Half-glaze sauce finished with mustard (6)
19. The floor waiter (6)
21. All the basic sauces are built up from this (4)
22. Best end without the 'é' (4)
24. . . . ordinaire (3)

Answers . . . .

1 Across

1 châteaubriand, 2 eel, 3 ananas, 4 dab, 5 appearance,
6 tronçon, 7 syrup, 8 guéridon, 9 cone, 10 fino, 11 brigade,
12 la, 13 oie, 14 sommelier, 15 in, 16 entrecôte, 17 cover

Down

1 chef d'étage, 9 carte, 18 ail, 19 edam, 20 bin, 21 nip,
22 mise-en-place, 23 aspic, 24 foie gras, 25 entrée, 26 cheese,
27 polivit, 28 oloroso, 29 ale, 30 foie, 31 inn, 32 à,
33 darne

2 Across

1 croûtons, 6 chop, 8 mango, 10 tabasco, 11 café, 12 beer,
13 rognons, 14 duplicate, 15 OP, 16 tuna, 17 chasseur,
20 oie, 21 rice, 23 Malvern, 25 Xérès, 26 tortue

Down

1 camembert, 2 tronc, 3 nip, 4 UP, 5 debarrasseur, 6 cos,
7 oloroso, 9 navet, 10 tequila, 14 darne, 16A ugli, 17 cigar,
18 robert, 19 d'étage, 21 roux, 22 carr, 24 vin